T0167982

Service,
Akathist,
Life and Miracles
of

Saint Nicholas
the
Wonderworker

Printed with the Blessing of
Archbishop Laurus
of Syracuse and Holy Trinity Monastery

© 1996 Holy Trinity Monastery,
all rights reserved.

Published by Holy Trinity Monastery, Jordanville,
N.Y. 13361-0036

Service,
Akathist,
Life and Miracles
of

Saint Nicholas *the* Wonderworker

SAINT NICHOLAS THE WONDERWORKER

SERVICE
To Our Father among the Saints, Nicholas the Wonderworker, Archbishop of Myra in Lycia

(Commemorated on December 6)

AT SMALL VESPERS:

At Lord I have cried, 4 stichera, Fourth Tone:
Prosomion: As valiant....

With divine myrrh* the divine grace of the Spirit anointed thee,* who didst preside as leader over Myra,* and having made the ends of the world fragrant with the myrrh of virtues* thou holiest of men,* through the pleasant breathings of thine intercessions* always driving away the evil stench of the passions.* Therefore, in faith we render thee great praise,* and celebrate thine all-holy memory, O Nicholas.

As an unwaning illuminator,* as a light to the whole world,* on the firmament of the Church* didst thou shine forth, O Nicholas,* enlightening the world,* and dispelling the fog of grievous adversity,* and taking away the sorrows of winter,* and making deep peace:* dutifully we bless thee.

Both here thou art, and revealing thyself in dreams, O Nicholas,* who didst save those unjustly condemned to death,* as a co-sufferer, as a lover of good things,* as a most fervent deliverer,* as a true intercessor* for those who in faith ask thy protection,* O most-holy Father,* fellow-citizen of the angels,* equal of the apostles and the prophets.

Thy marvellous life* everywhere hath shown thee to be most wondrous,* O godly-minded father most holy,* majesty of hierarchs,* adornment of the saints;* and as the rays of the sun spread abroad upon the earth,* hast thou shone into the hearts of the faithful,* who celebrate thy radiant and divine memory,* O all-blessed Nicholas.

Glory, Sixth Tone:

Thy memory which hath shone forth like the sun, O Hierarch, enlightening noetically the hearts of the faithful, we also, radiantly celebrate today, prayerfully crying unto thee: Rejoice, stronghold of chastity, thou didst keep the birthright of thy soul unenslaved, having armed thyself with the shield of continence. Rejoice, shepherd and teacher of thy people who bear Christ's name. Rejoice, adornment of the Church, glory of bishops, boast of monastics: O Saint Nicholas, all-blessed Father, entreat Christ God unceasingly, to grant peace to the world, and to save our souls.

Both now, theotokion

None that fleeth to thee departeth from thee ashamed, O most-pure Virgin Theotokos, but asketh grace, and receiveth a gift profitable according to his petition.

At the Aposticha, stichera, Sixth Tone.
Prosomion: On the third day Thou didst rise . . . .

O blessed Nicholas, show compassion to me who fall down praying to thee; and enlighten the eyes of my soul, O wise one, that I may clearly behold the Light-giver and Compassionate One.

Stichos: Precious in the sight of the Lord is the death of His saints.

From enemies seeking to do me evil, O holy one, rescue me, as thou art one having boldness before God, O Hierarch Nicholas, all-blessed one, and from men of blood do thou save me.

Stichos: Thy priests shall be clothed with righteousness, and Thy righteous shall rejoice.

A stormless haven and an invincible wall, O Hierarch, we faithful have acquired in thee, and a pillar of firmness, and a door of repentance, and a guide of souls, and a champion.

Glory, Both now, theotokion:

The adversary, being zealous against thy flock, O most-pure one, every day the evil one seeketh to make us food, but do thou, O Theotokos, rescue us from that harm.

Troparion, Fourth Tone:

The truth of things revealed thee to thy flock as a rule of faith, an icon of meekness and a teacher of temperance; therefore, thou hast achieved the heights by humility, riches by poverty. O Father and Hierarch Nicholas, intercede with Christ God that our souls be saved.

Glory, Both now, theotokion:

The mystery hidden from the ages, and unknown to angels, through thee, O Theotokos, is revealed to those on earth: God incarnate in union without confusion, and accepting the Cross voluntarily for our sake, by which, having raised the first-created man, He hath saved our souls from death.

At GREAT VESPERS

We chant Blessed is the man, the first antiphon. At Lord, I have cried, eight stichera, Second Tone.

Prosomion: When from the Tree....

Having dwelt bodily in Myra, thou wast truly shown forth as myrrh, having been anointed with noetic myrrh, O Saint Nicholas, hierarch of Christ; and thou dost ever make fragrant the faces of those who celebrate thine all-glorious memory with faith and love, loosing them from misfortune, and temptation, and affliction, O Father, by thine intercessions with God.

A namesake of victory, firm in the face of temptation, art thou truly shown to be to the faithful people, O Saint Nicholas, hierarch of Christ; for, called upon everywhere, thou dost quickly forestall them that hasten with love unto thy protection; for, manifesting thyself both day and night to the faithful, thou dost save from temptation and adversity.

Thou didst appear to Constantine the Emperor, and to Ablavius, in a dream, and putting fear into them, thus didst thou say: Loose at once then those held bound in prison, for they are innocent of lawless slaughter. Moreover, if thou shouldst disobey me, I will make petition against thee when I pray to the Lord.

A great and fervent helper art thou to those who find themselves in misfortune, O Saint Nicholas the glorious, holy preacher of Christ, to those on land and those who sail upon the sea, those found far and near, for an exceedingly compassionate and mighty intercessor art thou. Wherefore, having gathered together, we cry aloud: Entreat the Lord that we be delivered from adversity.

Other stichera, same tone.

Prosomion: With what crowns . . . .

ith what crowns of praise shall we crown the holy hierarch? Who was in Myra in the flesh, and reacheth out in spirit to all that fitly love him, the mediator and helper of all, and the comforter of all in affliction; and the refuge of all in misfortune, a pillar of piety, the champion of the faithful; for whose sake the arrogance of the enemy was laid low by Christ Who hath great mercy. Twice.

With what odes of song shall we praise the holy hierarch? Who was a fighter against ungodliness, and a champion of piety; a leader, a great protector and teacher of the Church, who put to shame all the ungodly; the destroyer of Arius and his supporters. For his sake their arrogance was laid low by Christ Who hath great mercy.

With what songs of the prophets shall we praise the holy hierarch? Who foresaw things afar off, and things distant as though they were near; who looked upon all the world, and delivered all from wrongs; who once appeared in a dream to the godly-minded emperor, and delivered the bound from an unjust execution, and grantest great mercy.

Glory, Sixth Tone:

The adornment of hierarchs, and the glory of the fathers, the fount of wonders and the great protector of the faithful, let us, O feast-lovers, having gathered together, hymn with songs of praise, saying: Rejoice, guardian of the people of Myra, and honored chief hierarch, and pillar immovable. Rejoice, all-radiant lamp that maketh the ends of the world shine with wonders. Rejoice, divine joy of those that sorrow, and fervent advocate of the wronged. And now, all-blessed Nicholas, cease not to entreat Christ God for those who with faith and love honor thine ever-gladdening and renowned memory.

Both now, of the Forefeast, same tone:

O cave, adorn thyself with majesty, for the Ewe Lamb cometh, bearing Christ in her womb; and do thou, O manger, receive Him Who by His word hath loosed us, who are born of earth, from irrational deeds. Ye shepherds piping in the fields, bear witness to the fearful wonder; and ye Magi from Persia, bring unto the King gold and frankincense and myrrh, for the Lord hath appeared from a Virgin Mother. Him, also, the Mother, bending over like a handmaiden, worshipped, and said to Him held in her embrace: How wast Thou sown in me, or how hast Thou budded in me, O my Redeemer and God?

Entry. Prokeimenon of the day. Three readings.

The Reading from Proverbs.

The memory of the righteous man is praised, and the blessing of the Lord is upon his head. Blessed is the man that findeth wisdom, and the mortal that getteth understanding. For it is better to obtain this than treasures of gold and silver. And she is more valuable than precious stones; no precious thing can be compared to her. For length of days and years of life are in her right hand, and in her left hand are wealth and glory. Out of her mouth proceedeth righteousness, and law and mercy she carrieth on her tongue. Hearken, then, unto me, O children, for I will speak excellent things; and blessed is the man that shall keep my ways; for my paths are the paths of life, and in them blessing is prepared of the Lord. Therefore, I exhort you, and utter my voice to the sons of men: for I wisdom have dwelt with counsel, and knowledge, and I have called forth understanding; counsel and safety are mine, understanding is mine, and strength is mine. I love them that love me, and they that seek me shall find grace. Understand subtlety, then, O ye simple, and ye uninstructed, incline your hearts to it. Hearken unto me again, for I will speak excellent things, and the opening of my mouth shall produce right things; for my throat shall meditate truth, and false lips are an abomination before me. All the words of my mouth are in righteousness; there is nothing in them wrong or perverse. They are all plain to him that understandeth, and right to them that find knowledge. For I will teach you the truth, that your hope may be in the Lord, and ye may be filled with the Spirit.

The Reading from Proverbs.

The mouth of the righteous droppeth wisdom, but the tongue of the unrighteous shall perish. The lips of righteous men drop grace, but the mouth of the ungodly is perverse. Dishonest scales are an abomination before the

Lord, but a just weight is acceptable unto Him. Wherever pride entereth, there shame entereth also; but the mouth of the lowly meditateth wisdom. The integrity of the upright shall guide them, and the overthrow of the rebellious shall save them. Possessions will not profit in a day of wrath, but righteousness will deliver from death. When a righteous man dieth, he leaveth regret; but the ruin of the ungodly is speedy and causeth joy. The righteousness of the blameless shall direct his way, but the unrighteous shall fall in their own wickedness. The righteousness of upright men delivereth them; but the lawless are caught in their own dishonesty. When a righteous man dieth, hope perisheth not; but the boast of the ungodly perisheth. A righteous man escapeth a snare, and the ungodly man is delivered up in his place. In the mouth of the ungodly is a snare to neighbours, but the understanding of righteous men is prosperous. In the prosperity of righteous men a city prospereth, and at the destruction of the wicked there is rejoicing. At the blessing of the upright a city shall be exalted, but by the mouths of ungodly men it is overthrown. He that is void of understanding revileth his neighbour, but a wise man holdeth his peace.

The Reading from the Wisdom of Solomon.

Though the righteous be overtaken by death, yet shall he be in rest. For honourable age is not in length of time, nor measured by length of years, but wisdom is gray hair unto men, and an unspotted life in old age. He pleased God, and was beloved of Him; so that living among sinners he was translated; he was taken up, lest that wickedness alter his understanding, or deceit beguile his soul. For the bewitching of evil doth obscure things that are good, and the wandering of lust doth undermine the simple mind. He, being made perfect in a short time, fulfilled a long time; for his soul was pleasing to the Lord; therefore He hastened to take him away from among the wicked. This the people saw, and understood not, neither did they lay this up in their minds, that grace and mercy is with His saints, and that He doth visit His chosen.

At the Litia, the sticheron of the temple; then stichera to Nicholas, Second Tone, idiomela:

By the Byzantine: A rule of faith and an icon of meekness did Christ God reveal thee to be to thy flock, O holy Hierarch Nicholas; for, while making Myra fragrant, as a protector of orphans and widows, everywhere thy divine deeds shine forth brightly. Wherefore, unceasingly entreat Him to save our souls.

O Father Nicholas, the myrrh-containing shrine of thy relics enricheth Myra, where, having appeared in a vision to the emperor, thou didst set free from death, and chains, and prison, those bound and unjustly condemned.

But also now, as then and ever, through visions dost thou reveal thyself, interceding for our souls.

O Father Nicholas, though the land of Myra be silent, yet the whole world which is enlightened by thee through the fragrance of myrrh and a multitude of wonders, shouteth hymns of praise; and with the condemned ones saved through thee, with those in Myra we also, chanting, cry aloud: pray that our souls be saved.

Fourth Tone: O Father Nicholas, a myrrh-containing shrine of the most Holy Spirit art thou, for in Myra thou dost diffuse a divine aroma; for, being like unto the apostles, thou goest throughout the world through word of thy wonders. Wherefore, to those afar thou appearest as near, manifesting thyself in dreams thou deliverest from death those unjustly condemned to die, unexpectedly saving from many dangers those who call upon thee. Wherefore, through thine intercessions do thou free from threatening evils us who ever praise thee.

Eighth Tone: The fruit of thy valourous deeds, O holy Father, hath enlightened the hearts of the faithful; for who, hearing of thy boundless humility, doth not wonder at thy patience, at thy kindness to the needy, at thy consolation to the afflicted? All didst thou teach in a godly manner, O holy Hierarch Nicholas, and now, crowned with an unfading crown, do thou intercede for our souls.

In praise of the Lord didst thou pass through the temporal life, O Nicholas, and He hath glorified thee in the heavenly and true life. Wherefore, having acquired boldness before Him, entreat Him to save our souls.

Glory, Sixth Tone:

O good and faithful servant, O labourer in the vineyard of Christ, thou didst both bear the burden of the day, and didst also increase the talent given thee; and thou didst not envy those who came after thee. Wherefore, the gates of heaven are opened to thee, enter thou into the joy of thy Lord, and pray for us, O Saint Nicholas.

Both now, same tone:

O Sion, triumph, O Jerusalem, be glad, city of Christ God, receive the Creator Who is contained in a cave and a manger; open to me the gates, and entering therein I shall behold a Child wrapped in swaddling clothes, Him Who holdeth creation in the palm of His hand; Him Whom the angels praise with unceasing voice, the Life-giver, the Lord, Who saveth our race.

At the Aposticha, stichera, Fifth Tone.
Prosomion: Rejoice . . . .

Rejoice! O sacred head, pure home of the virtues, example of the divine priesthood, name of victory, and merciful incliner to them that entreat him, who is disposed to listen to the petitions of the infirm, ready deliverer, saving guardian to all who with faith honour thine all-glorious memory: O most-blessed one, entreat Christ to send down upon the world great mercy.

Stichos: Precious in the sight of the Lord is the death of His saints.

Rejoice! O most sacred mind, pure dwelling of the Trinity, pillar of the Church, support of the faithful, help of the defeated, star by the shining of thine intercessions acceptable to God, always destroying temptations and the darkness of afflictions. O holy Hierarch Nicholas, peaceful haven in which the afflicted, fleeing the tumult of life, are saved: Do thou entreat Christ to grant our souls great mercy.

Stichos: Thy priests shall be clothed with righteousness and Thy righteous shall rejoice.

Rejoice! Thou who wast filled with divine zeal, and who, through dread appearance and warning in dreams, didst deliver from evil sentence those unjustly about to die; fountain that gusheth myrrh abundantly in Myra, O Nicholas, and sprinkling souls, dispelling the stench of passions; sword cutting off the tares of deception, fan winnowing out the weedy teachings of Arius. Do thou entreat Christ to send down upon our souls great mercy.

Glory, Sixth Tone:

By John the Monk: O man of God, and faithful servant, minister of the Lord, man worthy of love, chosen vessel, pillar and support of the Church, heir of the kingdom, do thou cease not to cry unto the Lord for us.

Both now, same tone.

By the Byzantine: O unwedded Virgin, whence camest thou? Who gave thee birth? Who was thy mother? How dost thou carry the Creator in thine arms? How was thy womb not corrupted? O great and marvellous and terrible mystery on earth we see accomplished in thee, O all-holy one; and we make ready thy worthy due, on earth a cave, and heaven we ask to give the star, and the Magi come from the land of the East to the West to see the Salvation of mankind, wrapped in swaddling clothes in a manger.

At the blessing of the breads the troparion, twice; written at Small Vespers; And O Theotokos and Virgin, once. And where there is no All-Night Vigil: at Great Vespers, after Now lettest Thou Thy servant, we say the troparion once:

Glory, Both now, and the Sunday theotokion.

AT MATINS,

at God is the Lord, troparion: The truth of things, twice.

Glory, Both now, theotokion: The mystery hidden from the ages;

After the first kathisma, the sessional hymn, First Tone:

Prosomion: Thy tomb . . . .

Living in Myra in the body, O hierarch, thou wast shown to be anointed wisely with the myrrh of spiritual wisdom, O Father Nicholas. Wherefore the myrrh of thy miracles hath filled the world with fragrance, pouring from myrrh ever-flowing, through word of the fragrance of thy myrrh, and thy memory.

Glory: Thou brightenest the earth with the rays of thy miracles, O wise Nicholas, and movest all nations to the glory and praise of Him Who hath glorified thee; entreat Him to deliver from all necessity those who honour thy memory with faith and love, O chosen among the fathers.

Both now, theotokion:

The Maker of all, the God and Creator,

didst thou, O all-blameless immaculate one, conceive in the womb by the Divine Spirit, and didst bear without corruption; Whom glorifying, we hymn thee, O Virgin, for thou art the palace of the King of all, and the defence of the world.

After the second kathisma, sessional hymn,
Fourth Tone:
Prosomion: Thou hast appeared ....

Thou makest intercession for the faithful, protecting, keeping them, O blessed one, plainly delivering them from all tribulation, O fairest glory and boast of hierarchs, Saint Nicholas.

Glory, Eighth Tone:
Prosomion: Of wisdom ....

Having received the source of miracles from the Lord, O wise Father, thou gushest forth honeyed waters for all the faithful, O blessed one; for as thou art a shepherd and preacher of the faith, thou didst fulfill the word of the True Shepherd. Wherefore, having boldness before Him, thou didst save people from death, O blessed Hierarch Nicholas. Entreat Christ God to grant remission of sins to those who with love honour thy holy memory.

Both now, theotokion:

I have fallen into the mire of sin, and for me there is no sure standing, and an evil tempest of sins hath overwhelmed me; but as thou hast borne the Word, the Only Lover of mankind, look upon me thy servant, and deliver me from all sins and soul-corrupting passions, and slay every vexation of the evil one, O pure, chaste Theotokos; entreat Christ God to grant me remission of sins, for I thy servant have thee as my hope.

After the Polyeleos, the sessional hymn, Fifth Tone:

Prosomion: Let us, O faithful....

Let us piously extol the most wise hierarch, the God-bearing Nicholas, for a fervent helper and defender from God is he in misfortune and tribulation; for he prayeth to the Lord for those who with faith make celebration and praise his divine memory.

Glory, Fourth tone:

Prosomion: Hasten to our aid....

A most fervent leader of the Church of Christ hast thou been shown to be, O Nicholas, and destroying the godless heresies with boldness, thou hast been revealed to all as a standard of Orthodoxy, praying for all that follow thy divine teachings and precepts.

Both now, theotokion:

Quickly receive our prayers, O Lady, and present these to thy Son and God, O Lady all-blameless; deliver from adversity those who hasten to thee; shatter the craftiness and cast down the daring of the godless who arm themselves, O most pure one, against Thy servants.

The hymn of ascents, first antiphon of the Fourth Tone.

Prokeimenon, Fourth Tone: Precious in the sight of the Lord is the death of His saints.

Stichos: What shall I render unto the Lord for all that He hath rendered unto me?
Let every breath; the Gospel of John, section 36 [10:9-16].

After the 50th Psalm, sticheron, Sixth tone:

O heir of God, O co-partaker of Christ, minister of the Lord, Saint Nicholas, according to thy name thus also was thy life; for thy wisdom shone forth with thy gray hair, the brightness of thy countenance bore witness to guilelessness of soul, the silent word testified of thy meekness. Thy life was renowned, and thy repose is with the saints: pray for our souls.

Canon to the Theotokos with eirmos, 6; And to the saint two canons, 8. The canon to the Theotokos, First Tone.

Ode I

Eirmos: Let us all sing a song of victory unto God, Who wrought marvellous wonders with His uplifted arm, and saved Israel, for He is glorified.

Thou who didst bear the Abyss of Wisdom, send down upon me drops of wisdom, O pure fount gushing with grace, that I may praise in song the depths of thy grace.

I praise thee, O all-hymned one, whom the ranks of angels praise in song; for thou gavest birth to God the supremely-praised, Whom all creation hymneth, for He is glorified.

Canon to the saint [of which the acrostic is: *To thee, O Nicholas, I chant a divine song*]. The work of Theophanes. Second Tone.

Ode I

Eirmos: In the deep of old the infinite Power overwhelmed Pharaoh's whole army, but the incarnate Word annihilated pernicious sin. Exceedingly glorious is the Lord, for gloriously is He glorified.

O crown-bearer, most-wise Nicholas, standing with the angelic hosts before the throne of Christ, grant me enlightenment, illumining the darkness of my soul, that with rejoicing I may extol thine all-blessed memory.

The Lord Who glorifieth all that glorify Him, hath given thee to the faithful as a refuge, O Nicholas, who deliverest from temptations those that flee to thy protection, and with faith and love call upon thee, O most glorious one.

Theotokion: Having put into me the desire to be equal to the Creator, the all-evil serpent hath taken me as a captive. But through thee, O all-pure one, I have been recalled, I have become truly godlike. For thou, O Mother of God, didst give birth to Him Who hath made me godlike.

Another canon, according to the alphabet except for the triadica and theotokia. First Tone.

Ode I

Eirmos: Christ is born, give ye glory; Christ from heaven, meet ye Him. Christ is on earth, be ye exalted. Sing unto the Lord all the earth, and in gladness sing praises, O ye people, for He is glorified.

With insufficient tongue and lips I have come to offer small praise and supplication, O Nicholas, to thy God-like excellence; but as thou art a giver of riches, give me the Saviour and God of mercies.

A heavenly man, and an equal to the angels on earth wast thou shown to be, a ready defender of widows, the avenger of the oppressed, and a helper to all the afflicted in misfortune, O Father Nicholas.

All things under the sun tell of thy wonders, O thrice-blessed Nicholas, and the depths of thy virtues: thou art a protector of the poor, and a nourisher of orphans and widows, a guide to the blind, and to all a defender.

Triadicon: The uncreated Trinity I venerate, the Father, and the Son with the Holy Spirit, simple essence, divinity, nature not severed in essence, three hypostases, dividing in person and according to hypostasis.

Theotokion: Seedlessly didst thou beget the Word, one of the Trinity, O all-blameless one, and Him didst thou bear in the flesh, remaining virgin after birth as thou wast also before; as He is thy Son and God, do thou ever pray to Him for us.

Katavasia: Christ is born . . . .

Ode III

Eirmos: Let my heart be strengthened in Thy will, O Christ God, Who hath established the second heaven above the waters, and hath founded the earth upon the waters, O Almighty One.

O purest heaven, habitation of the King, fragrant paradise truly breathing the breath of grace, O hope of Christians, my Mother of God I praise in song.

At a word didst thou bring forth the Word Who brought into being all rational nature, together with the irrational, delivering mankind from irrationality, O all-blessed one.

Another canon:

Eirmos: The desert blossomed like a lily at Thy coming, O Lord, to the barren church of the nations, in which my heart is strengthened.

O blessed Nicholas, having been an intimate disciple of the Master, thou savest those that flee unto thee from cruel dangers and bitter death.

Cleanse Thy servants, granting, as Thou art good, remission of sins, through the mediations of Thy servant Nicholas before Thee, O Thou Who art plenteous in mercy.

Theotokion: Assuage the disturbance of my soul, O most pure one, and pilot my life, O all-holy one, who didst give birth to God, in Whom my heart is strengthened.

Another canon:

Eirmos: To the Son begotten of the Father incorruptibly before the ages, and in latter times incarnate seedlessly of the Virgin, unto Christ God let us cry aloud: Thou hast lifted up our horn, holy art Thou, O Lord.

Having acquired in thy heart, O godly-wise one, a tablet of many virtues, written by the immortal and immaculate finger of Christ God, O Nicholas, thou pourest sweetness more sweet than honey and the honeycomb from thy mouth.

The grace on thee hath shown marvellous miracles, O Nicholas; for thy pure life truly brighter than gold shineth on dark souls with the radiance of the Divine Spirit.

Thou livest even after death, indeed appearing in dreams, and thou didst wondrously deliver the youths from death, clearly crying to the king: Wrong not these men, who have been slandered through vanity and envy.

Triadicon: Be merciful, O All-holy Trinity our God, to me who have defiled my life by countless transgressions, O Father, Son, and living Spirit, Who keepest me on all sides, and ever unwounded by tribulation.

Theotokion: Thou grantest, O Theotokos, the hope of salvation to thy servants, and in necessity and temptation thou standest ready to preserve and help with speedy intercessions; for thou art the boast of us believers, O Ever-virgin.

Katavasia: To the Son begotten . . . .

Sessional Hymn, Eighth Tone:
Prosomion: Of wisdom...

Having ascended on high from whence the divine effulgence of thy miracles and virtues, O father, hath shone forth, thou hast been revealed to the world as a true and most excellent shepherd, and to us in temptation thou art an invincible defender; wherefore, having wondrously vanquished the enemy, thou didst expel falsehood, and didst save men from death, O Nicholas. Entreat Christ God to grant remission of sins to those who lovingly honour thy holy memory.

Glory, another sessional hymn, same tone:

A river of healings abundantly pouring and a plentiful fountain of wonders hath the Abyss of mercy showed thee to be, O Nicholas; for those bitterly oppressed by illness, and those tormented by the cruel misfortunes of life truly find a healing remedy for every affliction, thy warm protection. Therefore we cry out to thee: pray to Christ God to grant remission of sins to those who with love festively celebrate thy holy memory.

Both now, theotokion:

As thou art virgin and the one among women who without seed gavest birth to God incarnate, we and all the race of man call thee blessed; for the Fire of Divinity dwelt in thee, and thou didst suckle the Creator and Lord as an infant. Wherefore, with the angels and the race of man we properly praise thy most holy birth-giving, and in harmony we cry out to thee: Entreat Christ God to grant remission of sins to those who with love worship thy holy birth-giving.

Ode IV

Eirmos: In the spirit foreseeing the incarnation of the Word, the Prophet Abbacum proclaimed, crying out: When the years draw nigh, Thou shalt be acknowledged, when the season cometh, Thou shalt be shown forth. Glory to Thy power, O Lord.

By the advice of the serpent Eve became the cause of death for earthly men; but thou, O pure Virgin, at a word having given birth to the Word, hast been revealed as a mediatress of life immortal. Wherefore meetly do we hymn thee.

In the spirit foreseeing thee, O pure one, as mountain, door, table, holy ark, lamp, throne of life, jar, and couch, Mother of God, the prophets revealed thee in riddles, of which we now see the fulfillment.

Another canon:

Eirmos: From a Virgin didst Thou come, not as an ambassador, nor as an angel, but the very Lord Himself incarnate, and didst save me the whole man. Wherefore, I cry to Thee: Glory to Thy power, O Lord.

Having clearly drawn near the rays of the Spirit, thou wast a light-bearer, enlightening the ends of the earth, interceding for all, and saving all that with faith flee unto thee.

As thou didst appear in former times, O Saint Nicholas, delivering the youths from death, thus also now save me from all adversity, and temptation and danger, O all-blessed one.

Thou didst shine forth with the radiance of the virtues, O all-blessed one, thou becamest a most excellent example of thy Master, and thou savest us who call upon thee, with reverence and love glorifying thee.

Theotokion: On thee came down incarnate the Master of creation, saving me the whole man, for He is compassionate; wherefore, we the faithful glorify thee, O Theotokos.

Another canon:

Eirmos: As the rod of the root of Jesse, and its flower, O Christ, Thou hast blossomed forth from the Virgin; out of a mountain overshadowed and densely wooded, O Praised One, hast Thou come, incarnate of one that knew not wedlock, O God Who art immaterial; Glory to Thy power, O Lord.

The mere invocation of thy name truly and speedily delivereth from all designs of the enemy those that fervently cry to thee, O Saint Nicholas; as thou didst before deliver the soldiers, save us also from all cruel adversity.

As thou standest before the throne of God, cease not to intercede fervently for all of us thy faithful servants, O wise and wondrous Nicholas, that we be delivered from the fire eternal, and from enemies, evil tongues, and oppression.

Healings dost thou gush forth everywhere for the faithful that flee unto thee and from bonds thou deliverest all. Wherefore, turn our sorrow into joy, through thy God-pleasing intercessions, O most-radiant Nicholas, laying low the pride of our enemies.

Triadicon: The principality of the unoriginate Godhead do I honour, the Father, and the Son, and the All-holy Spirit, do I venerate: the Maker of all things, unique, unsevered, three in character and ever divided into three Persons, one kingdom indivisible.

Theotokion: Thou truly art above earthly things and more honourable than the heavenly, thou alone, O Mother of God; for thou didst conceive in thy womb the Maker of all things, clothed in material flesh, Whom thou didst bear seedlessly. O strange wonder!

Katavasia: As the rod of the root of Jesse . . . .

Ode V

Eirmos: O Thou Who shinest forth brightly the light everlasting, we rise early for the judgments of Thy commandments, O Master, Lover of mankind, Christ our God.

As a precious ark of holiness, and as a holy throne in the likeness of fire, and as a sanctified palace, O Lady, thou didst contain the Almighty God.

O Mother who in virginity knew not man, a Virgin still in motherhood, O only most pure one, thou wast shown to be; for thou didst give birth ineffably to God Who restoreth nature.

Another canon.

Eirmos: O Enlightenment of those that lie in darkness, O Salvation of the despairing, Christ my Saviour, to Thee I wake at dawn, O King of peace; enlighten me with Thy radiance, for I know none other God beside Thee.

Enlightened through a divinely-majestic life, O thrice-blessed one, thou didst deliver, being present, those condemned to death through an unjust sentence, who cry to Christ the Master: For we know none other God beside Thee.

Now beholding in heaven the everlasting glory, and delighting in the inexpressible and divine rays of the brilliant effulgence, protect me with thine intercession, O saint, all-honourable servant of Christ.

Theotokion: That Thou mightest seek out Thine own image buried in passions, O Saviour, incarnate of the Virgin, hiding the mystery from the heavenly hosts, Thou didst appear to those that cry to Thee: We know none other God beside Thee.

Another canon:

Eirmos: As Thou art God of peace and Father of compassions, Thou hast sent unto us the Angel of Thy great counsel, granting peace unto us. Wherefore, having been guided unto light of the knowledge of God, out of the night waking, we glorify Thee, O Lover of mankind.

Thy wonders and miracles, O Father, the great city of Myra, and the diocese of Lycia, and all countries now proclaim; through them thou deliverest all from sickness and affliction, O God-blessed Nicholas.

Feeder of widows, and father of orphans, special helper of those in affliction, consolation of the grieving, shepherd and guide to all those astray art thou, O Nicholas, and do thou deliver us from misfortune through thine intercessions.

Thou wast translated from earth to the immaterial habitations, where thou beholdest the ineffable beauty of Christ, and hast appeared as a converser with the angelic hosts. Wherefore, rejoicing with the apostles and martyrs, fervently pray for us, O Father Nicholas, to the Master of all.

Triadicon: The co-unoriginate Three, one throne of the One indivisible Godhead, clearly sovereign Persons, I glorify. By Him I have been brought from non-being into being, and with the angels I cry: Holy, Holy, Holy, art Thou, O Lord.

Theotokion: O salvation and hope of all mankind, who alone hastenest to aid and save, help now also us who cry unto thee, O pure one, and who ever call upon thee in evil adversity: for after God we have no other mediator beside thee.

Katavasia: As Thou art God of peace....

Ode VI

Eirmos: Imitating the Prophet Jonah, I cry aloud: deliver my life from corruption, O Good One, and save me, O Saviour of the world, as I cry: Glory to Thee.

O protection of the faithful, and joyful gladness of the sorrowing, enrich with spiritual joy thy servants who desire thy protection.

Let the rational heaven, the most pure temple, the holy ark, the fairest paradise of God wherein was the Tree of my life, be praised.

Another canon.

Eirmos: Whirled about in the abyss of sin, I appeal to the unfathomable abyss of Thy compassion: from corruption raise me up, O God.

The crown of victory, O Nicholas, hath been worthily placed upon thy head; as a most noble victor, do thou save those who call upon thee.

O blessed one, revealing thyself, save me slain by sin and immersed by the violent storm of the passions, in the haven of the Divine will.

Theotokion: In thee, O Ever-Virgin Mother, I have placed my hope of salvation, and I make thee the firm and unshakable mediatress of my life.

Another canon.

Eirmos: The sea-monster spat forth Jonah as a babe from the womb, as it had received him; and the Word, having dwelt in the Virgin, and having taken flesh, came forth, preserving her incorrupt. For Himself having suffered not corruption, her that bare Him He kept unharmed.

As a new Abraham didst thou appear, O Nicholas, for thou didst bring as an only-begotten son unto thy Master the Bloodless Sacrifice, ever offering. Therefrom thou wast blessed for thy hospitality, O Father, and didst become a divine and blameless habitation of the Trinity.

Strange and dread wonders dost thou perform, O Nicholas, throughout the whole world, mediating for those in adversity far off at sea through thy swiftly-poured-out intercessions, a healer to the ailing, and a feeder of the needy, showing thyself to the faithful people as a namesake of victory against enemies.

With the eye of the mind foreseeing the future, thou hast filled all the ends of the earth with thy true teachings; declaring to us the Son to be of one essence with the Father, thou, O pillar of the Orthodox Faith, didst destroy the madness of Arius, having set forth thy precious instructions.

Triadicon: I honour and venerate the indivisible Trinity, ever divided into three Persons, yet united in essence and nature as One Principality, Father, and Son, and Holy Spirit, ruling all with power, and preserving all, as He willeth.

Theotokion: Entirely incarnate in thy womb, O most pure one, Christ God seedlessly was born; for not being able to endure the sight of the creation of His hands tormented by the deceiver, He came in the form of a servant to deliver the race of man.

Katavasia: The sea-monster spat....

Kontakion, Third Tone:
Prosomion: Today the Virgin....

In Myra, O Saint, thou didst prove to be a minister of things sacred: for, having fulfilled the Gospel of Christ, O righteous one, thou didst lay down thy life for thy people, and didst save the innocent from death. Wherefore, thou wast sanctified, as a great initiate of the grace of God.

Ekos: Let us now praise the hierarch in song, the shepherd and teacher of the people of Myra, that through his intercessions we may be enlightened; for behold, he hath appeared entirely pure, uncorrupt in spirit, offering to Christ the pure and blameless sacrifice acceptable to God, as a hierarch purified in soul and body. Wherefore, he is truly a leader and champion of this Church, as a great initiate of the grace of God.

Ode VII

Eirmos: The furnace, O Saviour, was bedewed, while the Children rejoicing sang: O God of our fathers, blessed art Thou.

The Most High showed thee to be heaven, a pure bridal chamber encircled with grace, purple sparkling like gold, and a living paradise.

Establish the inconstancy of my mind, strengthen my turbulent thoughts on an immovable rock by thy protection, O Virgin Mother.

Another Canon.

Eirmos: When the golden image was worshipped in the plain of Dura, Thy three children despised the godless order. Thrown into the fire, they were bedewed and sang: Blessed art Thou, O God of our fathers.

I have fallen on sharp temptation, and have been grievously pierced, and have drawn nigh unto the gates of hades, stricken with affliction; do thou save me through thine intercessions, O blessed one, and raise me up as I chant: Blessed art Thou, O God of our fathers.

O thou who shinest with the immaterial rays of the Unwaning Light, snatch the oppressed out of the darkness of affliction, and guide them to the enlightenment of gladness while they chant: Blessed art Thou, O God of our fathers.

Theotokion: Pray to Christ thy Son and God, O Virgin Mother of God, for those sold to grievous sins and the wiles of the serpent, that through His precious Blood they may be delivered who chant: Blessed art Thou, O God of our fathers.

Another canon.

Eirmos: The children brought up in piety, having scorned the impious decree, feared not the threat of fire, but standing in the midst of the flame they sang: O God of the fathers, blessed art Thou.

A most excellent physician of all grievous illnesses hast thou been shown to be, O Father Nicholas, having healed the infirmities of my soul, granting me perfect health to cry: O God of the fathers, blessed art Thou.

Having once delivered the soldiers from death, O Saint, thou didst move them to praise and glorify the Saviour Christ with ardent faith, and they cried: O God of the fathers, blessed art Thou.

Having mystically drawn nigh unto the cup of wisdom, O Father Nicholas, with thy lips thou didst draw out drops of ambrosia more sweet than honey and the honeycomb, commanding the people to cry: O God of the fathers, blessed art Thou.

Triadicon: O Trinity, we hymn Thee, One, Thrice-radiant, Single in Essence, Father, Son, and Holy Spirit, in Whom having been baptized, we all sing in praise: O God of the fathers, blessed art Thou.

Theotokion: As thou art higher than all creation, O Theotokos, entreat thy Son and God, that those who truly honour and glorify thee be delivered from torment. O God of the Fathers, blessed art Thou.

Katavasia: The children brought up in piety....

Ode VIII

Eirmos: Him Whom the hosts of angels fear as Creator and Lord, praise, O ye priests, glorify, O ye

Children, bless, O ye people, and supremely exalt Him unto all ages.

As a living bridal-chamber, and an animated crimson, a shining mantle of the King of all, adorned in purple, hast thou been shown to be, O Virgin, from whose flesh the Word shone forth, God and Man together.

Thou didst conceive, O most pure one, Him Who holdeth all creation in the hollow of His hand, Who as Creator and God ineffably and incomprehensibily for our sake became mortal man like us, and that which He was He did not cease to be.

Another canon.

Eirmos: O ye works, praise the Lord God, Who descended into the fiery furnace with the Hebrew children and changed the flame into dew, and supremely exalt Him unto all ages.

As thou art good and compassionate, free those held in the deep of grievous temptation, O blessed Nicholas, granting dispensation from grievous ills through thine intercessions to the Saviour Christ, O seer of sacred mysteries.

As thou art a leader into mysteries beyond understanding, a minister of things sacred and heavenly, and a faithful bishop, O godly-wise one, ask of our Saviour remission of sins, O herald of sacred mysteries.

Theotokion: My mind becometh now weak, having fallen into the deep of dishonour, for on all sides it is embraced by diverse evils. But do thou, O Virgin, heal it, covering it with the light of impassibility.

Another canon.

Eirmos: The dew-shedding furnace hath portrayed the image of a supernatural wonder; for as it scorched not the Youths whom it received, so neither did the fire of the Godhead singe the Virgin's womb which it entered. Wherefore, chanting praises, let us sing: Let all creation bless the Lord, and supremely exalt Him unto all ages.

The orders of the patriarchs, and the apostles, and the assemblies of hieromartyrs, and the choirs of prophets, all the assemblies of monastics call thy divine life blessed, and with them we also cry: Let all creation bless the Lord, and supremely exalt Him unto the ages.

O Most High and greatly-powerful King of all, through the intercessions of the holy shepherd, make the life of all Christians peaceful, O Word, giving our pious ruler(s) victory over barbarians, that we may cry to Thee, O Christ: Let all creation bless the Lord, and supremely exalt Him unto all ages.

Being enlightened by the Unapproachable Light, O Father, do thou illumine the souls of those in affliction, dispelling the gloom of dark temptations, shining gladness into our hearts, that with those enlightened by thy far-shining radiance we may cry: Let all creation bless the Lord, and supremely exalt Him unto all ages.

Triadicon: The Life and Lives, and One Light and Three Lights, the Trinity faithfully we praise in song, following the truly divine, patristic teaching, of the Father, and the Son, and the Holy Spirit. With which in piety let us cry: Let all creation bless the Lord, and supremely exalt Him unto all ages.

Theotokion: A wonder strangely majestic, the bush of old, burning without being consumed on Mount Sinai, was an image foreshadowing thee, O pure Maiden, mystically forefiguring thy child-birth: for in thee, keeping thee unharmed, dwelt the Divine Fire, of Whom we chant praises unto all ages.

Katavasia: The dew-shedding furnace....

Ode IX

Eirmos: The Life-receiving fountain ever-flowing, the Light-bearing lamp of grace, the living temple, the most pure tabernacle more spacious than heaven and earth, the Theotokos, do we faithful magnify.

Pour the stream of thy grace upon me, burnt by flames of evil fortune, languishing painfully, O fountain gushing grace, who gavest birth to the River of graces, whereof they that drink thirst nevermore.

As a beautiful bridal chamber, as the living palace of the Master, as all-golden purple, as the most beautiful abode of Christ, do thou, O Sovereign Lady of all, save me who implore thee.

Another canon.

Eirmos: The Son of the unoriginate Father, God and Lord, hath appeared to us incarnate of the Virgin, to enlighten those in darkness, and to gather the dispersed. Wherefore, the all-hymned Theotokos do we magnify.

Having been enlightened by the light of divine grace, and having truly been a lamp of piety, wondrously thou savest those in temptation, deliverest those in the depths of the sea, and feedest the hungry, O all-blessed one.

Dwelling in the paradise of delight, and clearly beholding the ineffable glory, from the vault of the heavens thou gazest upon thy praisers, delivering them from passions, O God-bearing all-blessed one.

Theotokion: The Wisdom, and Power, and hypostatic Word of the Father thou didst bear, O Mother of God; from thy most pure blood He took His Own temple, and to this He was united by an indivisible union.

Another canon.

Eirmos: A mystery strange and most glorious do I see: heaven, a cave; the throne of the cherubim, the Virgin; the manger, a container in which was laid the uncontainable Christ God, Whom praising we magnify.

We rejoice in spirit, all we feast-lovers; O ye heavens, be glad, ye mountains and hills, and ye churches and choirs of virgins, and radiance of fasters, in memory of the all-blessed one. Having come together for this, we magnify the Saviour.

Let all the ends of the earth chant with hymns unceasingly, with wreaths of praises openly adorning the head of Nicholas, the pleasing servant of Christ God; through whose intercessions may we be delivered from passions and dangers.

As a worthy song, O Nicholas, do thou receive this small effort, as Christ received the two mites of the widow; turn not away in loathing from one made wretched by passions, for, not priding myself, I have been bold, O thrice-blessed one.

Triadicon: United is the Trinity through the consubstantial will; and divided, yet indivisible in person, ever preserving the Sovereignty of the Father, Son, and living Spirit, one God in three Persons, Whom we magnify.

Theotokion: Every sorrow is destroyed through thy childbearing, and the Lord took away weeping and lamentation, and all tears from every face of those born of earth, O pure Theotokos who knew not wedlock. To thee also we render our due.

Katavasia: A mystery strange....

Exposteilarion.

Prosomion: Hearken, O ye women....

The great archpastor and hierarch, the chief bishop of Myra, Nicholas, let us all praise. For he saved many men who had been unjustly condemned to death, and to the king and

Ablavius he appeared in a dream, setting aside an unjust judgment.

Glory: Greatly hath the Lord glorified thee in wonders, in life and afterwards, O Hierarch Nicholas; for who out of love of the faith only calleth upon thy holy name, and is not heard at once, and doth not find thee a warm protector?

Both Now, Theotokion:

O Virgin who didst bear Christ the hypostatic Wisdom, and ever-existent Word, and the Physician of all, do thou heal the grievous and deep-rooted sores and wounds of my soul, and mortify the passionate thoughts of my heart.

At Lauds, 6 stichera, First Tone. Idiomela:

Having steadfastly looked upon heights of knowledge, and having beheld the hidden depths of wisdom, O father, thou didst enrich the world by thy teachings. Do thou ever pray to Christ for us, O holy Hierarch Nicholas.

O man of God and faithful servant, masterer of His mysteries, man of spiritual love, living pillar, and inspired image: the marvelling Church of Myra accepted thee as a divine treasury, and an intercessor for our souls.

Other stichera, same tone.

Prosomion: Rejoicing of the heavenly hierarchies....

Flying round the flowers of the Church, like a fledging from a nest of angels on high, O thrice-blessed Nicholas, thou dost ever cry to God for all of us who are in need, misforture, and temptation, and dost deliver us through thine intercessions.

The beauty of the priestly vestments thou didst make most bright with virtuous deeds through activity, O God-bearing Father. Wherefore, O Priest, thou dost perform for us wondrous miracles of renown through sacred functions, delivering us from misfortunes.

Having experienced the invisible beauty of the saints, thou didst understand that dread glory, O Saint. Wherefore, to us thou revealest heavenly words of those ever-living visions, O most-holy Father.

As in a dream thou didst appear to the pious emperor, and the prisoners, O Father, thou didst deliver from death, pray unceasingly that through thine intercessions they also now may be delivered from temptations and dangers and sickness who greatly praise thee as is meet.

Glory, Fifth Tone:

Let us sound the music of the trumpet, let us dance festally, rejoicing in prayerful celebration to the God-bearing father. Let kings and princes assemble, and let them praise him who by dread appearance in a dream persuaded the king to loose the three soldiers held without cause. Let the pastors and teachers of the Good Shepherd sing in praise; having come together let us extol the zealous shepherd. Praising the physician of those in sickness, and deliverer of those in misfortune, protector of sinners, treas-

ury of the poor, consolation of those in affliction, companion of those who journey, pilot of
those at sea, and the great hierarch who warmly
hasteneth to aid all everywhere, thus let us say:
O most-holy Nicholas, hasten and deliver us from
present dangers, and save thy flock through
thine intercessions.

Both now, theotokion, prosomion.
The work of Patriarch Germanus:

Let us sound the music of the trumpet: for,
looking down from on high, the Virgin Mother,
the Queen of all, with blessings crowneth those
that chant in praise of her. Let kings and
princes assemble, and let them clap their hands
in song to the Queen, who gave birth to the
King, Who in His love for mankind was pleased
to deliver those once held fast by death; O ye
pastors and teachers of the Good Shepherd,
having come together let us extol the most pure
Mother: the golden candlestick, the light-bearing
cloud, she who is more spacious than the heavens, the living ark, the fiery throne of the
Master, the manna-containing golden jar, the
closed-gate of the Word, the refuge of all Christians; with inspired songs boasting, thus let us
say: O palace of the Word, vouchsafe us lowly
ones the heavenly kingdom: for nothing is
impossible to thy mediation.

The Great Doxology. And the dismissal. And
the First Hour.

At the Liturgy:

Beatitude verses from the first canon, Ode III; and from the second canon, Ode VI.

Prokeimenon, Seventh Tone: The righteous man shall be glad in the Lord, and shall hope in Him. Stichos: Hearken, O God, unto my prayer, when I make supplication unto Thee. Epistle from Hebrews, section 335 [13:17-21]. Alleluia, Fourth Tone: Thy priests shall be clothed with righteousness, and Thy righteous shall rejoice. Gospel from Luke, section 24 [6:17-23]. Communion verse: In everlasting remembrance shall the righteous be; he shall not be afraid of evil tidings.

The reliquary of St. Nicholas, behind the screen.

AKATHIST
TO
SAINT NICHOLAS

Kontakion 1

O champion wonderworker and superb servant of Christ, thou who pourest out for all the world the most precious myrrh of mercy and an inexhaustible sea of miracles, I praise thee with love, O Saint Nicholas; and as thou art one having boldness toward the Lord, from all dangers do thou deliver us, that we may cry to thee:

Rejoice, O Nicholas, Great Wonderworker!

Ekos 1

An angel in manner though earthly by nature did the Creator reveal thee to be; for, foreseeing the fruitful beauty of thy soul, O most-blessed Nicholas, He taught all to cry to thee thus:

Rejoice, thou who wast purified from thy mother's womb!

Rejoice, thou who wast sanctified even unto the end!

Rejoice, thou who didst amaze thy parents by thy birth!

Rejoice, thou who didst manifest power of soul straightway after birth!

Rejoice, plant of the land of promise!

Rejoice, flower of divine planting!

Rejoice, virtuous vine of Christ's vineyard!

Rejoice, wonderworking tree of the paradise of Jesus!

Rejoice, lily of paradisaical growth!

Rejoice, myrrh of the fragrance of Christ!

Rejoice, for through thee lamentation is banished!

Rejoice, for through thee rejoicing is brought to pass!

Rejoice, O Nicholas, Great Wonderworker!

Kontakion 2

Seeing the effusion of thy myrrh, O divinely-wise one, our souls and bodies are enlightened, understanding thee to be a wonderful, living source of unction, O Nicholas; for with miracles like waters poured out through the grace of God thou fillest them that faithfully cry unto God: Alleluia!

Ekos 2

Teaching incomprehensible knowledge about the Holy Trinity, thou wast with the holy fathers in Nicea a champion of the confession of the Orthodox Faith; for thou didst confess the Son equal to the Father, co-everlasting and co-enthroned, and thou didst convict the foolish Arius. Therefore the faithful have learned to sing to thee:

Rejoice, great pillar of piety!

Rejoice, city of refuge for the faithful!

Rejoice, firm stronghold of Orthodoxy!
Rejoice, venerable vessel and praise of the Holy Trinity!
Rejoice, thou who didst preach the Son of equal honour with the Father!
Rejoice, thou who didst expel the demonized Arius from the council of the saints!
Rejoice, father, glorious beauty of the fathers!
Rejoice, wise goodness of all the divinely wise!
Rejoice, thou who utterest fiery words!
Rejoice, thou who guidest so well thy flock!
Rejoice, for through thee faith is strengthened!
Rejoice, for through thee heresy is overthrown!
Rejoice, O Nicholas, Great Wonderworker!

Kontakion 3

Through power given thee from on high thou didst wipe away every tear from the face of those in cruel suffering, O God-bearing Father Nicholas; for thou wast shown to be a feeder of the hungry, a superb pilot of those on the high seas, a healer of the ailing, and thou hast proved to be a helper to all that cry unto God: Alleluia!

Ekos 3

Truly, Father Nicholas, a song should be sung to thee from heaven, and not from earth; for how can a mere man proclaim the greatness of thy holiness? But we, conquered by thy love, cry unto thee thus:

Rejoice, model of lambs and shepherds!

Rejoice, holy purification of morals!

Rejoice, container of great virtues!

Rejoice, pure and honourable abode of holiness!

Rejoice, all-luminous lamp, beloved by all!

Rejoice, light golden-rayed and blameless!

Rejoice, worthy converser with angels!

Rejoice, good guide of men!

Rejoice, pious rule of faith!

Rejoice, model of spiritual meekness!

Rejoice, for through thee we are delivered from bodily passions!

Rejoice, for through thee we are filled with spiritual delights!

Rejoice, O Nicholas, Great Wonderworker!

Kontakion 4

A storm of bewilderment confuseth our minds: How can we worthily hymn thy wonders, O blessed Nicholas? For no one could count them, even though he had many tongues and willed to tell them; but we make bold to sing to God Who is wonderfully glorified in thee: Alleluia!

Ekos 4

People near and far heard of the greatness of thy miracles, O divinely-wise Nicholas, for in the air with the delicate wings of grace thou art accustomed to forestall those in misfortune, quickly delivering all who cry to thee thus:

Rejoice, deliverance from sorrow!

Rejoice, channel of grace !

Rejoice, dispeller of unexpected evils !

Rejoice, planter of good desires !

Rejoice, quick comforter of those in misfortune !

Rejoice, dread punisher of wrongdoers !

Rejoice, abyss of miracles poured out by God !

Rejoice, tablets of the law of Christ written by God !

Rejoice, strong uplifting of the fallen !

Rejoice, support of them that stand aright !

Rejoice, for through thee all deception is exposed !

Rejoice, for through thee all truth is realized !

Rejoice, O Nicholas, Great Wonderworker !

Kontakion 5

Thou didst appear as a divinely-moving star, guiding those who sailed upon the cruel sea who were once threatened with imminent death, if thou hadst not come to the help of those who called upon thee, O wonderworking Saint Nicholas; for, having forbidden the flying demons who shamelessly wanted to sink the ship, thou didst drive them away, and didst teach the faithful whom God saveth through thee to cry: Alleluia !

Ekos 5

The maidens, prepared for a dishonourable marriage because of their poverty, saw thy great compassion to the poor, O most-blessed

Father Nicholas, when by night thou secretly gavest their aged father three bundles of gold, thereby saving him and his daughters from falling into sin. Wherefore, thou hearest from all thus:

Rejoice, treasury of greatest mercy!

Rejoice, depository of provision for people!

Rejoice, food and consolation of those that flee unto thee!

Rejoice, inexhaustible bread of the hungry!

Rejoice, God-given wealth of those living in poverty on earth!

Rejoice, speedy uplifting of paupers!

Rejoice, quick hearing of the needy!

Rejoice, acceptable care of the sorrowful!

Rejoice, blameless provider for the three maidens!

Rejoice, fervent guardian of purity!

Rejoice, hope of the hopeless!

Rejoice, delight of all the world!

Rejoice, O Nicholas, Great Wonderworker!

Kontakion 6

The whole world proclaimeth thee, O most-blessed Nicholas, as a quick intercessor in adversities; for, oftentimes preceding those that travel by land and sail upon the sea, thou helpest them in a single hour, at the same time keeping from evils all that cry unto God: Alleluia!

Ekos 6

Thou didst shine as a living light, bringing deliverance to the generals who received sentence to an unjust death, who called upon thee, O good shepherd Nicholas, when thou didst quickly appear in a dream to the emperor, and didst terrify him and didst order him to release them unharmed. Therefore, together with them we also gratefully cry unto thee:

Rejoice, thou who helpest them that fervently call upon thee!

Rejoice, thou who deliverest from unjust death!

Rejoice, thou who preservest from false accusation!

Rejoice, thou who destroyest the counsels of the unrighteous!

Rejoice, thou who tearest lies to shreds like cobwebs!

Rejoice, thou who gloriously exaltest truth!

Rejoice, release of the innocent from their fetters!

Rejoice, revival of the dead!

Rejoice, revealer of righteousness!

Rejoice, exposer of unrighteousness!

Rejoice, for through thee the innocent were saved from the sword!

Rejoice, for through thee they enjoyed the light!

Rejoice, O Nicholas, Great Wonderworker!

Kontakion 7

Desiring to dispel the blasphemous stench of heresy, thou didst appear as a truly fragrant, mystical myrrh, O Nicholas; by shepherding the people of Myra, thou hast filled the whole world with thy gracious myrrh. And so, dispel from us the stench of abominable sin, that we may acceptably cry unto God. Alleluia!

Ekos 7

We understand thee to be a new Noah, a guide of the ark of salvation, O holy Father Nicholas, who drivest away the storm of all evils by thy direction, and bringest divine calm to those that cry thus:

Rejoice, calm harbor of the storm-tossed!

Rejoice, sure preservation of those that are drowning!

Rejoice, good pilot of those that sail upon the deeps!

Rejoice, thou who rulest the raging of the sea!

Rejoice, guidance of those in whirlwinds!

Rejoice, warmth of those in frosts!

Rejoice, radiance that dispellest the gloom of sorrow!

Rejoice, light that illuminest all the ends of the earth!

Rejoice, thou who deliverest people from the abyss of sin!

Rejoice, thou who castest Satan into the abyss
of hades!

Rejoice, for through thee we boldly invoke
the abyss of God's compassion!

Rejoice, for, as ones rescued through thee
from the flood of wrath, we find
peace with God!

Rejoice, O Nicholas, Great Wonderworker!

Kontakion 8

A strange wonder is thy sacred church shown
to be to those that flock to thee, O blessed
Nicholas; for, by offering in it even a small
supplication, we receive healing from great illnesses, if only, after God, we place our hope in
thee, faithfully crying aloud: Alleluia!

Ekos 8

Thou art truly a helper to all, O God-bearing
Nicholas, and thou hast gathered together
all that flee unto thee, for thou art a deliverer, a
nourisher, and a quick healer to all on earth,
moving all to cry out in praise to thee thus:

Rejoice, source of all kinds of healing!

Rejoice, helper of those that suffer cruelly!

Rejoice, dawn shining for prodigals in the
night of sin!

Rejoice, heaven-sent dew for those in the heat
of labours!

Rejoice, thou who givest prosperity to those
that need it!

Rejoice, thou who preparest an abundance for those that ask!

Rejoice, thou who often forestallest requests!

Rejoice, thou who restorest strength to the aged and gray-headed!

Rejoice, convicter of many who have strayed from the true way!

Rejoice, faithful steward of the mysteries of God!

Rejoice, for through thee we conquer envy!

Rejoice, for through thee we lead a moral life!

Rejoice, O Nicholas, Great Wonderworker!

Kontakion 9

Assuage all our pains, O Nicholas, our great intercessor, dispensing gracious healings, delighting our souls, and gladdening the hearts of all that fervently hasten to thee for help and cry unto God: Alleluia!

Ekos 9

The falsely-theorizing orators of the ungodly, we see, were put to shame by thee, O divinely-wise Father Nicholas; for thou didst confute Arius the blasphemer who divided the Godhead, and Sabellius who mingled the persons of the Holy Trinity, but thou hast strengthened us in Orthodoxy. Therefore we cry unto thee thus:

Rejoice, shield that defendest piety!

Rejoice, sword that cuttest down impiety!

Rejoice, teacher of the divine commandments!

Rejoice, destroyer of impious doctrines!

Rejoice, ladder set up by God, by which we mount to heaven!

Rejoice, God-given protection, by which many are sheltered!

Rejoice, thou who makest wise the unwise by thy sayings!

Rejoice, thou who movest the slothful by thine example!

Rejoice, inextinguishable brightness of God's commandments!

Rejoice, most luminous ray of the Lord's statutes!

Rejoice, for through thy teaching the heads of heretics are broken!

Rejoice, for through thee the faithful are counted worthy of glory!

Rejoice, O Nicholas, Great Wonderworker!

Kontakion 10

Desiring to save thy soul, thou didst truly subject thy body to the spirit, O our Father Nicholas; for by silence first and by wrestling with thoughts, thou didst add contemplation to activity, and by contemplation thou didst acquire perfect knowledge with which thou didst boldly converse with God and angels, always crying: Alleluia!

Ekos 10

Thou art a rampart, O most-blessed one, to those that praise thy miracles, and to all

that have recourse to thine intercession; wherefore, free also us who are poor in virtue from
poverty, temptations, illness, and needs of
various kinds, as we cry unto thee thus:

Rejoice, thou who rescuest from eternal
wretchedness!

Rejoice, thou who bestowest incorruptible
riches!

Rejoice, imperishable food for those that
hunger after righteousness!

Rejoice, inexhaustible drink for those that
thirst for life!

Rejoice, thou who preservest from revolution
and war!

Rejoice, thou who freest us from chains and
imprisonment!

Rejoice, most-glorious intercessor in misfortunes!

Rejoice, great defender in temptations!

Rejoice, thou who hast snatched many from
destruction!

Rejoice, thou who hast kept countless num-
bers unharmed!

Rejoice, for through thee sinners escape a
frightful death!

Rejoice, for through thee those that repent
obtain eternal life!

Rejoice, O Nicholas, Great Wonderworker!

Kontakion 11

A song to the Most Holy Trinity didst thou bring, surpassing others in thought, word, and deed, O most-blessed Nicholas; for with much searching thou didst explain the precepts of the true Faith, guiding us to sing with faith, hope, and love to the one God in Trinity: Alleluia!

Ekos 11

We see thee as a brilliant and inextinguishable ray for those in the darkness of this life, O God-chosen Father Nicholas; for with the immaterial angelic lights thou conversest concerning the uncreated Light of the Trinity, and thou enlightenest the souls of the faithful who cry unto thee thus:

Rejoice, radiance of the Three-sunned Light!
Rejoice, daystar of the unsetting Sun!
Rejoice, lamp kindled by the Divine Flame!
Rejoice, for thou hast quenched the demonic flame of impiety!
Rejoice, bright preaching of the Orthodox Faith!
Rejoice, luminous radiance of the light of the Gospel!
Rejoice, lightning that consumest heresy!
Rejoice, thunder that terrifiest tempters!
Rejoice, teacher of true knowledge!
Rejoice, revealer of the secret mind!

Rejoice, for through thee the worship of creatures hath been abolished!

Rejoice, for through thee we have learned to worship the Creator in the Trinity!

Rejoice, O Nicholas, Great Wonderworker!

Kontakion 12

Knowing the grace that hath been given thee by God, dutifully and joyfully we celebrate thy memory, O most-glorious Father Nicholas, and with all fervency we hasten to thy wonderful intercession; unable to count thy glorious deeds which are like the sands of the seashore and the multitude of the stars, being at a loss to understand, we cry unto God: Alleluia!

Ekos 12

While we sing of thy wonders, we praise thee, O all-praised Nicholas; for in thee God Who is glorified in the Trinity is wondrously glorified. But even if we were to offer thee a multitude of psalms and hymns composed from the soul, O holy wonderworker, we should do nothing to equal the gift of thy miracles, and amazed by them we cry unto thee thus:

Rejoice, servant of the King of kings and Lord of lords!

Rejoice, co-dweller with His heavenly servants!

Rejoice, support of faithful kings!

Rejoice, exaltation of the race of Christians!

Rejoice, namesake of victory!

Rejoice, eminent victor!

Rejoice, mirror of all the virtues!

Rejoice, strong buttress of all who flee unto thee!

Rejoice, after God and the Theotokos, all our hope!

Rejoice, health of our bodies and salvation of our souls!

Rejoice, for through thee we are delivered from eternal death!

Rejoice, for through thee we are deemed worthy of endless life!

Rejoice, O Nicholas, Great Wonderworker!

Kontakion 13

O most-holy and most-wonderful Father Nicholas, consolation of all that sorrow, accept our present offering, and entreat the Lord that we be delivered from Gehenna through thy God-pleasing intercession, that with thee we may sing: Alleluia! *This kontakion is read thrice.*

And again Ekos 1 and Kontakion 1:

Ekos 1

An angel in manner though earthly by nature did the Creator reveal thee to be; for, foreseeing the fruitful beauty of thy soul, O most-blessed Nicholas, He taught all to cry to thee thus:

Rejoice, thou who wast purified from thy mother's womb!

Rejoice, thou who wast sanctified even unto
the end!

Rejoice, thou who didst amaze thy parents by
thy birth!

Rejoice, thou who didst manifest power of
soul straightway after birth!

Rejoice, plant of the land of promise!

Rejoice, flower of divine planting!

Rejoice, virtuous vine of Christ's vineyard!

Rejoice, wonderworking tree of the paradise
of Jesus!

Rejoice, lily of paradisaical growth!

Rejoice, myrrh of the fragrance of Christ!

Rejoice, for through thee lamentation is
banished!

Rejoice, for through thee rejoicing is brought
to pass!

Rejoice, O Nicholas, Great Wonderworker!

Kontakion 1

O champion wonderworker and superb servant of Christ, thou who pourest out for all the world the most precious myrrh of mercy and an inexhaustible sea of miracles, I praise thee with love, O Saint Nicholas; and as thou art one having boldness toward the Lord, from all dangers do thou deliver us, that we may cry to thee:

Rejoice, O Nicholas, Great Wonderworker!

PRAYER
to
Saint Nicholas

O all-praised and all-honoured hierarach, great wonderworker, saint of Christ, Father Nicholas, man of God and faithful servant, man of love, chosen vessel, strong pillar of the Church, most-brilliant lamp, star that illuminest and enlightenest the whole world: thou art a righteous man that didst flourish like a palm tree planted in the courts of the Lord; dwelling in Myra thou hast diffused the fragrance of myrrh, and thou pourest out the ever-flowing myrrh of the grace of God. By thy presence, most-holy Father, the sea was sanctified when thy most-miraculous relics were carried to the city of Bari, from the East to the West to praise the name of the Lord. O most-superb and most-marvellous wonderworker, speedy helper, fervent intercessor, good shepherd that saveth the rational flock from all dangers, we glorify and magnify thee as the hope of all Christians, a fountain of miracles, a defender of the faithful, a most wise teacher, a feeder of the hungry, the gladness of those that mourn, clothing of the naked, healer of the sick, pilot of those that sail the sea, liberator of prisoners, nourisher and protector of widows and orphans, guardian of chastity, gentle tutor of children, support of the aged, guide of fasters, rest of those that labour, abundant riches of the poor and needy. Hearken unto us that pray unto thee and flee to thy protection, show thy mediation on our behalf with the Most High, and obtain through thy God-pleasing intercessions all that is useful for the salvation of our souls and bodies; keep this holy habitation (*or* this temple), every city and town, and every Christian country, and the people that dwell therin, from all oppression through thy help; for we know, we know that the prayer of a righteous man availeth much for good; and after the most-blessed Virgin Mary, we have thee as a righteous mediator with the All-Merciful God, and to thy fervent intercession and protection we humbly hasten. Do thou, as a watchful and good shepherd, keep us from all enemies, pesilence, earthquake, hail, famine, flood, fire, the sword, the invasion of aliens, and in all our misfortunes and afflictions do thou give us a helping hand and open the doors of God's compassion; for we are unworthy to look upon the height of heaven because of the multitude of our unrighteousnesses; we are bound by the bonds of sin and have not done the will of our Creator nor kept His commandments. Wherefore, we bow the knees of our broken and humble heart to our Maker, and we ask thy fatherly intercession with Him: Help us, O servant of God, lest we perish with our sins, deliver us from all evil, and from every adverse thing, direct our minds and strengthen our hearts in the Orthodox Faith, which, through thy mediation and intercession, neither wounds, nor threats, nor plague, nor the wrath of our Creator shall lessen; but vouchsafe that we may live a peaceful life here and see the good things in the land of the living, glorifying the Father, and the Son, and the Holy Spirit, one God glorified and worshipped in Trinity, now and ever, and unto the ages of ages. Amen.

Byzantine Icon of the XIVth Century

The LIFE of
The Holy Hierarch and Wonderworker
NICHOLAS
Archbishop of Myra in Lycia

Commemorated on December 6

The holy hierarch of Christ, Nicholas, the great wonderworker, a speedy helper and an extraordinary mediator before God, grew up in the land of Lycia. He was born in the town of Patara.[1] His parents, Theophanes and Nonna, were pious people, prominent and wealthy. This blessed couple, for their God-pleasing life, many alms and great virtues, were worthy to raise a branch holy and *like the tree which is planted by the streams of the waters, which shall bring forth its fruit in its season.*[2] When this blessed youth was born, he was given the name *Nicholas*, which means *conqueror of nations*. And he, by the blessing of God, truly appeared as a conqueror of evil, for the good of the whole world. After his birth, his mother Nonna was immediately free of pain and from that time until her death remained barren. By this nature itself bore witness that this woman could not have another son, similar to St. Nicholas: he alone should be the first and the last. Sanctified already while in his mother's womb by the grace of God, he showed himself to be a reverent venerator of God before he saw the light of day; he began to perform miracles earlier than he began to feed on his mother's milk, and was a faster before he was accustomed to eat food. After his birth, while still in the baptismal font, he stood on his feet for three hours, supported by no one, by this rendering honor to the Holy Trinity, of Whom he later would show himself to be a great servitor and intercessor. In him it was possible to recognize the future wonder-worker even by the way in which he drew near to his mother's breast, because he fed on the milk only of the right breast, signifying by this his future standing on the right hand of the Lord together with the righteous. He gave signs of his extraordinary abstinence in that on Wednesdays and Fridays he took his mother's milk only once, and this in the evening, after the parents' completion of the customary prayers.

His father and mother were much astonished and foresaw what a strict faster their son would be in his life. Being accustomed to such temperance from his swaddling clothes, St. Nicholas during his whole life until his death spent Wednesday and Friday in strict fasting. Growing with the years, the youth grew also in knowledge, perfecting himself in the virtues, in which he was taught by his pious parents. And he was like a fruitful field, receiving in itself and putting forth the good seed of instruction and bringing forth every day new fruits of good behavior. When the time came to learn the divine Scriptures, St. Nicholas, by the force and acuteness of his mind and the help of the Holy Spirit, in a little time attained much wisdom and succeeded in book-learning such as befits a good pilot of Christ's ship and a skillful shepherd of rational sheep. Having reached perfection in word and learning, he showed himself to be perfect in his very life. He by all means avoided vain friends and idle conversations, shunning conversation with women and didn't even look at them. St. Nicholas preserved a true chastity, with a pure mind always contemplating on the Lord and assiduously visiting the temple of God, following the Psalmist, who said: *I have chosen rather to be an outcast in the house of my God.*[3] In the temple of God he passed entire days and nights in lifting up his mind to God in prayer and in the reading of divine books, meditating on spiritual knowledge, enriching himself in the divine grace of the Holy Spirit and creating in himself a worthy dwelling for Him, in accordance with the words of the Scripture: *Ye are the temple of God and the Spirit of God dwelleth in you.*[4] The Spirit of God indeed dwelt in this virtuous and pure youth and, serving the Lord, he glowed with the Spirit. In him were noticed no habits natural to youth: in his moral disposition he was like an old man, because all esteemed him and marvelled at him. An old man, if he shows youthful inclinations is a laughing-stock to everyone; on the other hand, if a youth has the disposition of an old man, he is esteemed by all with wonder. Inappropriate is youth in old age, but excellent and worthy of esteem is old age in youth.

St. Nicholas had an uncle, bishop of the town of Patara, having the same name as his nephew who was called Nicholas in his honor. This bishop, seeing that his nephew was successful in the virtuous life and by all means evaded the world, began to advise his parents that they should give their son to the service of God. These heeded this advice and consecrated to the Lord their child whom they themselves had received from Him as a gift. For in ancient books it is told concerning them that they were childless and already had no hope of having children, but by many prayers, tears, and deeds of mercy they begged of God a son for themselves, and now had no regret in bringing him as a gift to Him Who had given him. The bishop, receiving this old man in youth, who had *gray hairs of wisdom and youth in old age, an undefiled life,*[5] raised him to the rank of priest. When he ordained St. Nicholas a priest, then, by the inspiration of the Holy Spirit, addressing the people who were in the church, he pronounced a prophecy:

"I see, brethren, a new sun rising above the earth and manifesting in himself a gracious consolation for the afflicted. Blessed is the flock that will be worthy to have him as its pastor, because this one will shepherd well the souls of those who have gone astray, will nourish them on the pasturage of piety, and will be a merciful helper in misfortune and tribulation."

This prophecy was indeed later fulfilled, as will be evident from later narrative.

Having accepted the priestly rank, St. Nicholas added labors to labors; keeping vigil and remaining in unceasing prayer and fasting, he, being mortal, strove to imitate the bodiless ones. Leading a life equal to the angels and flowering from day to day all the more in beauty of soul, he was entirely worthy to rule in the church. At this time, Bishop Nicholas, desiring to go to Palestine for the veneration of the holy places, handed over the rule of the church to his nephew. This priest of God, St. Nicholas, having taken over the place of his uncle, took care of the affairs of the church in the same way as the bishop himself. At this time his parents passed on to eternal life. Having obtained their estate in inheritance, St. Nicholas distributed it to the needy. For he paid no attention to temporal riches and did not concern himself with its increase, but, renouncing all earthly desires, with all his heart he strove to devote himself to the One God, crying: *Unto Thee, O Lord, have I lifted up my soul. Teach me to do Thy will, for Thou art my God. On Thee was I cast from the womb; from my mother's womb, Thou art my God.*[6]

And his hand was outstretched to the needy, on whom it poured alms richly, as a water-filled river abounds in streams. Here is one of his many deeds of mercy.

There lived in the town of Patara a certain man, prominent and rich. Falling into extreme poverty, he lost his former prominence, because of the uncertain life of this age. This man had three daughters who were very beautiful in appearance. When he was already deprived of all necessities, so that there was nothing to eat and nothing to wear because of his great poverty, he planned to give his daughters to prostitution and turn his house into a brothel so that by this means he might obtain a livelihood for himself and acquire also food and clothing for himself and his daughters. O woe! To such unworthy thoughts does extreme misery lead! Having this unclean thought this man wanted already to fulfill his evil design. But the All-good Lord, not desiring to see a man in perdition and, in His love for mankind, helping in our misfortunes, placed a good thought in the mind of His servant, the holy priest Nicholas, and by inspiration sent him secretly to the man who was perishing in soul, for consolation in poverty and forewarning from sin. St. Nicholas, having heard of the extreme poverty of this man and knowing through revelation from God of his evil intention, felt great pity for him and decided to draw him out, together with his daughters, from poverty and sin, as from fire. However, he did not wish to show his good deed to this man openly, but intended to give generous alms secretly. St. Nicholas did thus for two reasons. On the one hand, he wanted to escape vain, human glory, following the words of the Gospel: *Take heed that ye do not your alms before men*;[1] on the other hand, he did not want to offend the man who once was rich and now had fallen into extreme poverty. For he knew how painful and insulting alms are to him who has fallen into pauperism, because it reminds him of his former prosperity. Therefore St. Nicholas considered it better to act according to the teaching of Christ: *Let not thy left hand know what thy right hand doeth.*[8] He so much shunned the praise of men that he tried to hide himself even from him whom he benefitted. He took a large sack of gold, came at midnight to the house of that man and, throwing this sack in the window, hastened to return home. In the morning this man arose and, finding the sack, untied it. At the sight of gold, he fell into great consternation and did not believe his eyes, because from nowhere could he expect such a favor. However, in examining the money with his fingers, he was convinced that it was in fact gold before him. Having rejoiced in spirit and wondering at it, he wept for joy, for a long time he pondered over who could show him such a favor, and could think of nothing. Attributing this to the action of divine providence, he continually thanked his benefactor in his soul, rendering praise to the Lord Who cares for all. After this he gave his oldest daughter in marriage, giving her as dowry the gold miraculously given to him. St. Nicholas, knowing that this man acted according to his wishes, loved him and decided to do a like mercy also to the second daughter, intending by a lawful wedding to protect her also from sin. Preparing another sack of gold like the first one, he by night, hidden from all, by the same window threw it into the house of man. Arising in the morning, the poor man again found gold in his house. Again he was astonished and, falling to the earth and drenching himself with tears, he said:

"O merciful God, Author of our salvation, Who hast redeemed me by Thine Own Blood and now redeemest by gold my home and my daughters from the nets of the enemy, do Thou Thyself show me the minister of Thy mercy and Thy philanthropic goodness. Show me this earthly angel who preserves us from sinful perdition, so that I might know who hath snatched us from the poverty which oppresses us and delivers us from evil thoughts and intentions. O Lord, by Thy mercy secretly done for me by the generous hand of Thy servant unknown to me, I can give my second daughter lawfully in marriage and with this escape the snares of the devil, who desired by a tainted gain, or even without it, to increase my great ruin."

Having prayed thus to the Lord and having thanked Him for His goodness, this man celebrated the wedding of his second daughter. Hoping in God, the father nourished undoubting hope that He would also grant a lawful husband to the third daughter, again secretly giving by a beneficent hand the gold necessary for it. In order to learn who brought gold to him, and whence, the father did not sleep for many nights, watching for his benefactor and desiring to see him. Not much time passed when the awaited benefactor appeared. The servant of Christ, Nicholas, quietly came also a third time and, having stopped at the usual place, threw in the same window a similar sack of gold, and immediately hurried to his home. Hearing the clink of the gold thrown in the window, the man ran after the servant of God as rapidly as possible. Having caught up with him and recognizing him, because it was impossible not to know the saint by his virtues and illustrious origin, the man fell at his feet, kissing them and calling the saint a deliverer, a helper, and a saviour of souls which came to the edge of ruin.

"If," said he, "the Lord great in mercy had not raised me up through thy generosity, then I, an unfortunate father, already long ago would be lost together with my daughters in the fire of Sodom. Now we are saved through thee and delivered from a horrible fall into sin."

And yet many similar words he tearfully said to the saint. Just after raising him from the earth, the holy servant of God took from him an oath that during his life he would tell no one about what had happened to him. Telling him yet many things to his profit, the saint dismissed him to his home.

Out of the many deeds of mercy of the servant of God we have related only one, so that it be known how merciful he was to the poor. Because there would not be enough time for us to tell about this in detail, how generous he was to the destitute, how many hungry he fed, how many naked he clothed, and how many he ransomed from money-lenders.

After this, the holy father Nicholas desired to go to Palestine, to see and venerate those holy places where our Lord God, Jesus Christ, walked with His most pure feet. When the ship sailed near Egypt and the travelers knew not what awaited them, St. Nicholas, who was among them, foresaw that soon a storm would arise and informed his fellow travelers of it, telling them that he had seen the devil himself entering the ship with the intent to drown all of them in the depths of the sea. And in this very hour unexpectedly the heavens were covered with clouds, and a powerful storm raised a terrible turbulence on the sea. The travelers fell into great terror, and having despaired of their salvation and expecting death, entreated holy father Nicholas to help them who were perishing in the deep sea.

"If thou, O servant of God," they said, "do not help us by thy prayers to the Lord, then we shall immediately perish."

Commanding them to have courage, to place their hope in God and without any doubts to expect a speedy deliverance, the saint began to pray fervently to the Lord. Immediately the sea became peaceful, and a great calm set in, and the common sorrow turned into joy. The joyful travelers rendered thanksgiving to God and His servant, holy Father Nicholas, and were doubly astonished — both at his foretelling of the storm and the cessation of distress. After this, one of the sailors had to climb to the top of the mast. In descending from there he slipped and fell from the very heights to the middle of the ship, killing himself and lying breathless. St. Nicholas, ready to help before it was needed, at once resurrected him by his prayer, and the man rose as if awaking from sleep. After this, hoisting all sails, the travelers happily continued their voyage, under favorable winds, and peacefully put in to shore at Alexandria. Healing here many ill and demon-possessed people and consoling the afflicted, the servant of God St. Nicholas again set out for Palestine according to his original plan.

Reaching the holy city of Jerusalem, St. Nicholas came to Golgotha, where Christ our God stretched out His immaculate hands and wrought salvation for the race of mankind. Here God's servant poured out prayers from a heart burning with love, sending up thanksgiving to our Saviour. He went round all the holy places, making fervent veneration everywhere. And when at night he wanted to enter a holy church[9] for prayer, the closed doors of the church swung open by themselves, disclosing an unhindered entry to him for whom were opened also the heavenly gates. Having spent a long enough time in Jerusalem, St. Nicholas intended to seclude himself in the desert, but was restrained by a Divine voice from on high, which admonished him to return to his homeland. The Lord God Who orders everything to our profit, did not will that that luminary, who by the will of God needs must illuminate the metropolis of Lycia, should remain hidden under a bushel in the desert. Having arrived aboard ship, the servant of God made an agreement with the crew so that they would deliver him to his native land. But they schemed to deceive him and directed their ship not to Lycia, but to another land. When they sailed from the harbor, St. Nicholas, noticing that the ship sailed another way, fell at the feet of the seamen, beseeching them to direct the ship to Lycia. But they paid not the slightest attention to his entreaties and continued to sail along the charted route: they didn't know that God would not forsake His servant. And suddenly a storm swooped down, turned the ship in the other direction, and quickly carried it in the direction of Lycia, threatening the crew with complete destruction. Thus carried by Divine power over the sea, St. Nicholas finally arrived in his fatherland. In his good nature he did no evil to his perfidious enemies. He not only was not angry, but also did not accuse them by a single word, but dismissed them with a blessing to their own country. He himself came to the monastery founded by his uncle and called Holy Sion, and here he proved to be a welcome guest to the entire brotherhood. Receiving him with great love as an angel of God, they were delighted by his divinely-inspired speech and, imitating the good nature with which God had adorned His servant, learned from his angel-like life. Finding in this monastery a silent life and a peaceful haven for contemplation, St. Nicholas hoped also to spend the remaining time of his life here without going out. But God showed him a different way, because He did not desire so rich a treasure of virtue, which ought to enrich the world, to remain cloistered in a monastery, like a treasure buried in the earth, but that it should be open to all and by him accomplish a spiritual purchase, acquiring many souls. And so, once, the saint, standing at prayer, heard a voice from on high:

"Nicholas, if you desire to be vouchsafed a crown from Me, go and struggle for the good of the world."

Hearing this, St. Nicholas was terrified and began to ponder over what this voice desired and required of him. And again he heard:

"Nicholas, here is not the field on which you must bring forth the fruit I expect; but turn back and go into the world and let My name be glorified in you."

Then St. Nicholas realized that the Lord needed him to forsake the podvig of silence and go into the service of people for their salvation.

He began to consider where he should go, either to his fatherland, the town of Patara, or to another place. Fleeing vainglory among his fellow citizens and fearing it, he thought of removing himself to another town where no one would know him. In this same Lycian land was the renowned city of Myra, which was the metropolis of all Lycia.[10] To this city came St. Nicholas, led by divine providence. Here he was known to no one; and he remained in this city as a pauper, having nowhere to lay his head. Only in the house of the Lord did he find shelter, having his only refuge in God. At that time the bishop of this city, John, the archbishop and foremost hierarch of the entire land of Lycia, died. Consequently all the bishops of Lycia gathered in Myra in order to choose a worthy one for the vacant throne. Many respected and prudent men were nominated as successors to John. Among those who were doing the choosing there was a great discord, and certain among them, led by Divine zeal, said:

"The election of a bishop to this throne is not up to the decision of people, but is a matter of God's direction. It is proper for us to say prayers so that the Lord Himself will disclose who is worthy to receive such rank and be the shepherd of the whole land of Lycia."

This good counsel met with general approval and all devoted themselves to fervent prayer and fasting. The Lord Who fulfills the desires of those that fear Him, attending to the prayer of the bishops then revealed to the oldest of them His good will. When this bishop stood at prayer, before him appeared a man in an image of light and commanded him to go to the doors of the church during the night and observe who will enter before everyone else.

"This," said He, "is My choice; receive him with honor and install him as archbishop; the name of this man is Nicholas."

The bishop informed the rest of the bishops about such a divine vision, and these, hearing this, increased their prayers. The bishop who had been considered worthy of the revelation stood in that place where it was ordered in the vision, and awaited the coming of the desired man. When the time came for the morning service, St. Nicholas, urged by the spirit, came to the church before all, for he was accustomed to rise at midnight for prayer and come earlier than the others for the morning service. As soon as he entered the narthex, the bishop who had been vouchsafed the revelation stopped him and asked him to tell his name. St. Nicholas remained silent. The bishop again asked him about his name. The saint meekly and softly answered him:

"My name is Nicholas, I am the servant of thy holiness, Master."

The pious bishop, hearing such a brief and humble speech, understood by the very name — Nicholas — foretold him in vision, as well as by the humble and meek answer, that before him was the very man whom God was pleased to have as foremost bishop of the church of Myra. For he knew from Holy Scripture that the Lord takes care of the meek, the silent, and those who tremble before the word of God. With great joy he rejoiced, as if he had received some secret treasure. Immediately taking St. Nicholas by the hand, he told him:

"Follow me, child."

When with honor he led the saint to the bishops, they were filled with divine delight, and being relieved in spirit that they had found the man indicated by God Himself, they conducted him to the church. Rumor about this spread everywhere and innumerable multitudes of people flocked swifter than birds to the church. The bishop who had been deemed worthy of the vision addressed the people and exclaimed:

"Brethren, receive your shepherd whom the Holy Spirit Himself anointed and to whom He entrusted the care of your souls. He was not appointed by an assembly of men, but by God Himself. Now we have the one that we desired, and have found and accepted the one we sought. Under his rule and instruction we will not lack the hope that we will stand before God in the day of His appearing and revelation."

All the people gave thanks to God and rejoiced with ineffable joy. Not being able to endure the praise of men, for a long time St. Nicholas refused to accept the sacred office; but yielding to the ardent requests of the council of bishops and all the people, he ascended the episcopal throne against his will. To this he was impelled by a Divine vision which he had yet before the death of Archbishop John. Concerning this vision St. Methodius, patriarch of Constantinople, relates. Once — he said — St. Nicholas saw at night that before him stood the Saviour in all His glory and gave him a Gospel ornamented with gold and pearls. On the other side of himself St. Nicholas saw the most holy Theotokos who placed on his shoulders the episcopal omophorion. After this vision a few days passed, and Archbishop John of Myra died.

Recalling this vision and seeing in it the clear will of God, and not wishing to refuse the fervent entreaties of the council, St. Nicholas accepted the flock. The council of bishops with all the church clergy performed over him the ordination and joyously celebrated, made glad by the shepherd given of God, Nicholas, the hierarch of Christ. By this means the Church of God received a bright lamp which did not remain under a bushel, but was set on the episcopal and pastoral place proper to him. Having been honored with this great office, St. Nicholas rightly divided the word of truth and wisely guided his flock in the teaching of faith.

In the beginning of his pastorship the servant of God said to himself thus:

"Nicholas! The rank received by you requires different habits, so that you live not for yourself, but for others."

Desiring to instruct his rational sheep in the virtues, he did not hide his virtuous life as before. For formerly, he passed his life secretly serving God Who Alone knew his ascetic feats. But now, after receiving the episcopal office, his life was open to all, not by vainglory before the people, but for their benefit and the increase of God's glory, so that the word of the Gospel be fulfilled: *"Let your light so shine before men that they may see your good works and glorify your Father Who is in heaven.*[11] By his good deeds St. Nicholas was like a mirror for his flock and, according to the word of the apostle, *"an example of the believers, in word, in conversation, in love, in spirit, in faith, and in purity.*[12] In character he was meek and forgiving, humble of spirit, and shunned all vainglory. His clothing was simple, his food — fasting fare, which he always ate only once a day, and that in the evening. All the day long he spent in labor proper to his office, listening to the requests and needs of those who came to him. The doors of his house were open to all. He was kind and affable to all, to orphans he was a father, to the poor a merciful giver, to the weeping a comforter, to the wronged a helper, and to all a great benefactor. To assist in him in the ruling of the church he chose two virtuous and prudent counselors who were invested with priestly rank. These were men well-known in all of Greece — Paul of Rhodes and Theodore of Ascalon.

So St. Nicholas tended the flock entrusted to him, the rational sheep of Christ. But the envious evil serpent, never ceasing to incite war against the servants of God and not enduring the flourishing of piety among the people, raised persecution against the Church of Christ through the impious emperors Diocletian and Maximian.[13] At this same time, from these emperors an order was sent all over the empire that Christians must renounce Christ and worship idols. Those who did not submit to this order were compelled to it by confinement in prison and severe tortures and, finally, given over to execution. This storm breathing evil, by the fervor of the zealots of darkness and ungodliness, soon reached also the city of Myra. The blessed Nicholas, who was the leader of all Christians in this city, freely and boldly preached the piety of Christ and was ready to suffer for Christ. For this he was seized by impious torturers and confined in prison together with many Christians. He remained not a little time, bearing severe suffering, enduring hunger and thirst and an overcrowded dungeon. He fed his fellow prisoners on the word of God and quenched their thirst with the water of piety; confirming in them faith in Christ God, strengthening them on an indestructible foundation, he persuaded them to be firm in the confession of Christ and to suffer eagerly for the truth. By this time Christians again were given freedom, and piety shone forth, like the sun after dark storm clouds, and like some calm coolness after a storm. For Christ the Lover of mankind, looking upon His inheritance, annihilated the ungodly, casting down Diocletian and Maximian from the imperial throne and destroying the power of the adherents of Hellenic impiety. By the appearance of His Cross to Constantine the Great, to whom He was pleased to entrust the kingdom of Rome, the Lord God *"raised up a horn of salvation"*[14] for His people. The Emperor Constantine, recognizing the One God and placing all his hope in Him, conquered all his enemies by the power of the precious Cross and ordered all temples of idols to be destroyed and Christian temples to be restored, and dispelled the vain hopes of his predecessors. He liberated all confined in prisons for Christ, and honoring them with great praises as courageous warriors, returned these confessors of Christ each to his fatherland. At this time also the city of Myra again received its shepherd, the great bishop Nicholas, who had been deemed worthy of the crown of martyrdom. Bearing in himself the Divine grace, he, as before, healed the passions and ailments of people, and not only of the faithful, but also the unbelievers. Because of the great grace of God that dwelt in him, many glorified him and were astonished at him and all loved him. For he shone with purity of heart and was endowed with all the gifts of God, serving his Lord in holiness and righteousness. At that time there remained still many Hellenic temples, to which impious people were attracted by devilish suggestion and many inhabitants of Myra remained in perdition. The archbishop of the Most High God, animated by Divine zeal, visited all these places, destroying and turning into dust the temples of the idols and purifying his flock from diabolical defilement. Thus fighting with evil spirits, St. Nicholas came to the temple of Diana,[15] which was very large and richly adorned, presenting an agreeable dwelling for demons. St. Nicholas destroyed this polluted temple, leveled its high edifice to the ground and the very foundation of the temple, which was in the earth, he scattered in the air, taking up arms more against the demons than against the temple itself. The evil spirits, not enduring the arrival of the servant of God, uttered doleful cries, but, vanquished by the weapon of prayer of the unconquerable warrior of Christ, St. Nicholas, they were forced to flee from their habitation.

The right-believing Emperor Constantine, desiring to firmly establish the Christian Faith, commanded an ecumenical council to be convened in the city Nicea. The holy fathers of the council laid down the correct teaching, anathematized the Arian heresy, and together with it Arius[16] himself, confessing the Son of God of equal honor and essence co-everlasting with the Father, re-established peace in the holy Divine, Apostolic Church. St. Nicholas was also among the 318 fathers of the council. He stood courageously against the impious teachings of Arius, and together with the holy fathers of the council affirmed and taught all the dogmas of the Orthodox Faith. A monk, John, of the Studite Monastery relates concerning St. Nicholas that, animated like the Prophet Elias by zeal for God, he put the heretic Arius to shame at the council not only by word but also by deed, smiting him on the cheek. The fathers of the council were indignant at the saint and for his daring action decided to deprive him of his episcopal rank. But our Lord Jesus Christ Himself and His most-blessed Mother, beholding from on high the deed of St. Nicholas, approved His courageous action and praised his divine zeal. For some of the holy fathers of the council had a vision similar to the one the saint himself was vouchsafed even before his ordination to the episcopate. They saw that on one side of the saint stands Christ the Lord Himself with the Gospel, and on the other, the most pure Virgin Theotokos with an omophorion, and they give the hierarch the emblems of his rank, of which he was deprived. Understanding from this that the boldness of the saint was pleasing to God, the fathers of the council ceased to reprove the saint and rendered him honor as a great servant of God.[17] Returning from the council to his flock, St. Nicholas brought it peace and blessing. With his mellifluous mouth he taught the entire people sound instruction, cut off at the very root erroneous ideas and reasonings and, having exposed the embittered, senseless heretics deep-rooted in wickedness, expelled them from Christ's flock. As a wise farmer purifies all that is found on the threshingfloor or on a grindstone, selects the best grain, and plucks out the tares, so the prudent laborer on the threshingfloor of Christ, St. Nicholas, filled the spiritual granary with good fruit, scattered and swept away the tares of heretical deception from the wheat of the Lord. That is why the Holy Church calls him a fan blowing away the weedy teachings of Arius. And indeed he was a light for the world and salt of the earth, because his life was light and his words were salted with wisdom. This good shepherd took great care for his flock, in all of its needs, not only nourishing it on spiritual pasturage, but also providing for its bodily needs.

Once in the land of Lycia there was a great famine, and in the city of Myra there was an extreme shortage of food. Feeling pity for the unfortunate people who were perishing from hunger, God's bishop appeared at night in a dream to a certain merchant who happened to be in Italy, who loaded his entire ship with grain and intended to sail to another land. Giving him a pledge of three gold coins, the saint commanded him to sail to Myra and sell the grain there. Awaking and finding the gold in his hand, the merchant was frightened, amazed by such a dream which was accompanied by the miraculous appearance of money. The merchant did not dare to disobey the command of the saint, went to the city of Myra and sold out his bread to its inhabitants. At the same time he did not hide from them the appearance of St. Nicholas to him in a dream. Having acquired such consolation in hunger and listening to the tale of the merchant, the citizens gave glory and thanks to God and extolled their miraculous nourisher, the great Bishop Nicholas.

At that time in great Phrygia there arose a revolt. Having learned of it, the Emperor Constantine sent three commanders with their soldiers to pacify the rebellious region. These were the commanders Nepotian, Ursus, and Herpylion. With great haste they set sail from Constantinople and remained at one port of the diocese of Lycia which was called the Adriatic shore. Here there was a town. Since strong rough seas prevented their sailing farther, they remained in this harbor to wait for calm weather. During their stay certain soldiers, going ashore to purchase necessities, took a great deal by force. Since this happened often, the inhabitants of this town were embittered; as a consequence, at a place called Plakomata, there arose argument, strife, and abuse between them and the soldiers. Learning of this, the holy Bishop Nicholas himself decided to travel to that town in order to quell the civil strife. Hearing of his arrival, all the citizens, together with the soldiers, went out to meet him and bowed down. The saint asked the commanders whence and whither they guarded the way. They told him that they were sent by the emperor to Phrygia to put down the revolt which had arisen there. The saint admonished them to hold their soldiers in submission and not to allow them to oppress the people. After this he invited the commanders into the city and cordially entertained them. The commanders, having disciplined the offending soldiers, stilled the revolt, and were honored with a blessing from St. Nicholas. When this happened, there arrived from Myra certain citizens lamenting and weeping. Falling at the feet of the saint, they asked him to defend the wronged, relating to him with tears that in his absence the ruler Eustathius, bribed by envious and evil people, condemned to death three men from their town, who were guilty of no crime.

"Our whole town," they said, "laments and weeps, and awaits your return, Master. For if you had been with us, then the ruler would not have dared to make such an unjust judgement."

Having heard about this, God's bishop began to grieve in soul, and in company with the commanders immediately set out on his way. Upon reaching the place, called "Leo," the saint met certain travelers and asked them whether they knew of those men condemned to death. They answered:

"We left them on the field of Castor and Pollux, being dragged away to execution."

St. Nicholas went faster, rushing to prevent the death of those innocent men. Having reached the place of execution, he saw that a multitude of people was gathered there. The condemned men, with their arms bound crosswise and with faces covered, had already knelt on the ground, stretched out their bare necks and awaited the blow of the sword. The saint saw that the executioner, harsh and violent, had already drawn his sword. Such a spectacle threw all into horror and distress. Combining anger with meekness, Christ's saint passed freely among the people, without any fear snatched the sword from the hands of the executioner, threw it upon the ground and then set the condemned men free of their bonds. All this he did with great boldness, and no one dared to stop him, because his word was powerful and Divine power was apparent in his actions: he was great before God and all the people. The men, delivered from the death sentence, seeing themselves unexpectedly restored from near death to life, shed warm tears and uttered joyful cries, and the all the people assembled there gave thanks to their bishop. The ruler Eustathius arrived there and wanted to approach the bishop. But the servant of God turned away from him with disdain and when the ruler fell at his feet, he thrust him aside. Calling down upon him the vengeance of God, St. Nicholas threatened him with torment for his unjust rule and promised to tell the emperor of his deeds. Being denounced by his own conscience and frightened by the threats of the bishop, the ruler with tears begged for mercy. Repenting of his injustice and desiring reconciliation with the great Father Nicholas, he laid his guilt before the elders of the city, Simonides and Eudocius. But the lie could not be hid, because the bishop knew well that the ruler, being bribed with gold, condemned the innocent to death. For a long time the ruler begged him to forgive him, and only then, when, with great humility and tears he acknowledged his sin, did the servant of Christ grant him forgiveness.

At the sight of all that happened, the commanders who had remained together with the hierarch were amazed at the zeal and goodness of the great bishop of God. Having been vouchsafed of his prayers, and having received from him a blessing for their journey, they set out for Phrygia in order to fulfill the royal command given to them. Arriving at the place of the revolt, they quickly suppressed it, and having fulfilled the royal commission, they returned with joy to Byzantium. The emperors and all the grandees gave them great praise and honor, and they were deemed worthy to take part in the royal council. But evil people envying such fame of the commanders, conceived enmity against them. Having meditated evil against them, they came to Eulavius, the ruler of the city, and slandered those men, saying:

"The commanders counsel ill, because, as we have heard, they introduce innovations and meditate evil against the emperor."

In order to win over the ruler to their side, they gave him much gold. The ruler informed the emperor. Having heard about this, the emperor, without any investigation, ordered those commanders to be confined in prison, fearing that they might run away secretly and fulfill their evil design. Languishing in jail, and conscious of their innocence, the commanders were perplexed as to why they were thrown in prison. After a short time, the slanderers began to fear that their slander and evil would come to light and they themselves might suffer. Therefore, they came to the ruler and fervently begged him that he not allow those men to live so long and hasten to condemn them to death. Ensnared in the nets of avarice, the ruler was obliged to carry out what was promised to the end. He immediately departed to the emperor and, like a messenger of evil, appeared before him with a sad face and a sorrowful look. Along with this, he wished to show that he was very much concerned about the life of the emperor and truly devoted to him. Striving to incite the emperor's anger against the innocent, he began to hold forth with lying and cunning speech, saying:

"O Emperor, not one of those shut in prison wishes to repent. All of them persist in their evil design, not ceasing to plot intrigues against you. Therefore, command without delay to hand them over to torture, so that they may not anticipate us and accomplish their evil deed, which they planned against the military commanders and you."

Alarmed by these words the emperor immediately condemned the commanders to death. But because it was evening, their punishment was delayed until morning. The prison guard learned of this. Having privately shed many tears over such a disaster threatening the innocent, he went to the commanders and said to them:

"For me it would have been better if I had not known you and had not enjoyed pleasant conversation and repast with you. Then I would easily bear separation from you and would not lament in soul over the disaster coming upon you. Morning will come, and the final and horrible separation will overtake us. I already do not see your faces dear to me, and do not hear your voice, because the emperor ordered to execute you. Instruct me how to deal with your possessions while there is yet time, and death has not yet prevented you from expressing your will."

He interrupted his speech with sobs. Learning of their horrible sentence, the generals rent their clothing and tore their hear, saying:

"What enemy has begrudged us our lives? For the sake of what are we, like malefactors, condemned to execution? What have we done, for what is it necessary to hand us over to death?"

And they called upon their relatives and friends by name, setting God Himself as their witness, that they had done no evil, and wept bitterly. One of them by the name of Nepotian recalled, regarding St. Nicholas, how he, having appeared in Myra as a glorious helper and good defender, delivered three men from death. And the commanders began to pray:

"O God of Nicholas, having delivered the three men from an unjust death, look now also upon us, for there can be no help from men. There hath come upon us a great disaster, and there is none who might deliver us from disaster. Our voice is cut off before the departure of our soul from the body, and our tongue is parched, burnt up by the fire of our heartfelt distress, so that we are not able to offer prayer unto Thee. *Let Thy compassions quickly go before us, O Lord.*[18] *Rescue us out the hand of them that seek after our souls.*" Tomorrow they wish to kill us, but do Thou hasten to our aid and deliver us innocent ones from death."

Attending to the prayers of those who fear Him and, like a father, pouring out compassion on His children, the Lord God sent His saint and servant, the great Bishop Nicholas, as help to the condemned men. That night the saint of Christ appeared to the emperor in a dream and said:

"Arise quickly and release those commanders languishing in prison. They were slandered to you and they suffer guiltlessly."

The saint explained in detail every deed and added:

"If you do not obey me and do not let them go, then I will raise a revolt against you similar to the one that occurred in Phrygia and you will perish by an evil death."

Astounded at such boldness, the emperor began to wonder how this man dared to enter into the inner chamber at night, and said to him:

"Who are you that you dare to threaten us and our power?"

He replied: "My name is Nicholas, I am the bishop of the metropolis of Myra."

The emperor became confused and, arising, began to ponder upon what this vision meant. Meanwhile, on that night the saint appeared to the ruler Eulavius and informed him about the condemned men also. Awakening from sleep, Eulavius became frightened. While he thought on this vision, there came a messenger from the emperor and told him about what the emperor had seen in a dream. Hastening to the emperor, the ruler disclosed his vision to him, and both of them were amazed that they had seen one and the same thing. At once the emperor ordered the commanders brought to him from prison, and said to them:

"By what sorcery did you bring these dreams upon us? A very angry man appeared to us and threatened us, boasting to soon bring war upon us."

The commanders turned one to another in perplexity and, knowing nothing, looked at one another with distressed glances. Noticing this, the emperor was mollified and said:

"Fear no evil, tell the truth."

With tears and sobs they replied:

"O Emperor, we know nothing of sorcery and have designed no evil against your power, may the All-seeing Lord be a witness in this. If we are deceiving you, and you learn anything ill of us, then allow no favor or clemency either to us or to our relatives. From our fathers we learned to honor the emperor and be faithful to him before all things. Thus also now we faithfully defend your life and, as is proper to our rank, unswervingly fulfill your commands to us. Serving you with zeal, we subdued the revolt in Phrygia, stopped the civil strife, and demonstrated our courage sufficiently by this deed itself, as those witness to whom this is well-known. Your power heaped honors upon us before, and now you with anger set yourself against us and pitilessly condemned us to an agonizing death. And so, O Emperor, we think that we suffer only for our zeal toward you alone, for which we have been condemned and, instead of glory and honors which we had hoped to receive, the fear of death has overtaken us."

At this address the emperor became compassionate and repented of his rash behavior. For he began to tremble before the judgement of God and felt embarrassment for his royal purple, seeing that he, being a lawgiver for others, was ready to make a lawless judgment. He looked compassionately upon the condemned men and conversed with them briefly. Listening to his speech with compunction, the commanders suddenly saw St. Nicholas sitting next to the emperor and, by signs, promising him forgiveness. The emperor interrupted their discourse and asked:

"Who is this Nicholas, and which men did he save? Tell me about it."

Nepotian related to him everything in the order of its occurrence. Then the emperor, learning that St. Nicholas was a great servant of God, marvelled at his boldness and his great zeal in defense of the wronged, freed those commanders and said to them:

"It is not I that grant you life, but the great servant of the Lord, Nicholas, whom you called upon for help. Go to him and offer him thanksgiving. Say to him also from me that 'I fulfilled your command that the servant of Christ be not angry with me.'"

With these words he handed them a golden Gospel, a golden censer ornamented with stones, and two lamps and ordered all this to be given to the church of Myra. Having received a miraculous escape, the commanders set out on their way at once. Arriving in Myra, they rejoiced and were glad that they were vouchsafed to see the saint again. They expressed great gratitude to St. Nicholas for his wonderful help and chanted:

"Lord, O Lord, who is like unto Thee? Delivering the beggar from the hand of them that are stronger than he." [19]

They gave generous alms to the needy and the paupers and returned home safely.

Such are the works of God with which the Lord magnified His servant. The fame of them spread everywhere, as on wings, it reached across the sea and spread throughout the world, so that there was no place where people did not know of the great and wonderful miracles of the great bishop Nicholas, which he wrought by the grace given him by the Almighty Lord.

Once, travelers sailing by ship from Egypt to the land of Lycia encountered strong turbulent seas and storm. The sails were already torn by the hurricane, the ship was lashed by the blows of the waves, and all despaired of their deliverance. At this time they remembered the great bishop Nicholas, whom they had never seen but only heard of, that he is a speedy helper to all that call upon him in misfortune. They turned to him in prayer and began call upon him for aid. The saint immediately appeared to them, walked on to the ship, and said:

"You called upon me, and I have come to help you; be not afraid!"

All saw that he took the helm and began to pilot the ship. As on that occasion when our Lord bade the winds and the sea,[20] the saint at once commanded the storm to cease, keeping in mind the words of the Lord:

"He that believeth on Me, the works that I do shall he do also."[21]

Thus the true servant of the Lord commanded both the wind and the sea, and they were obedient to him. Afterwards, under favorable winds the travelers reached the city of Myra. Going ashore they went to the city, desiring to see him who had saved them from disaster. They met the saint on the way to church and, recognizing in him their benefactor, they fell at his feet, giving thanks to him. The wondrous Nicholas not only delivered them from danger and death, but also showed concern for their spiritual salvation. By his clairvoyance he saw in them with his spiritual eyes the sin of fornication, which separates man from God and leads him away from keeping the commandments of God, and said to them:

"Children, I beseech you, consider within yourselves and correct your hearts and thoughts for the pleasing of the Lord. For even if we have hidden things from many people and have reckoned ourselves righteous, yet nothing can be hidden from God. Therefore, hasten with all diligence to preserve sanctity of soul and purity of body. For thus saith the divine Apostle Paul: *"Ye are the temple of God . . . if any man defile the temple of God, him shall God destroy.*"[22]

Having instructed those men with edifying words, the saint dismissed them in peace. For the character of the saint was as a child-loving father, and his countenance shone with Divine grace like an angel of God. From his face, as from the face of Moses, emanated a bright ray, and to him who only looked at him there was great benefit. For him who was burdened with some kind of passion or affliction of soul, it was enough to fix his gaze on the saint in order to receive consolation in his sorrow; and he who conversed with him already improved in good. And not only Christians, but also non-believers, if any of them came to hear the sweet and mellifluous discourses of the saint, came to compunction and, noting the evil of unbelief which was implanted in them since infancy and accepting in their heart the right word of truth, entered upon the way to salvation.

The great servant of God lived for many years in Myra, shining with Divine goodness, in the words of the Scripture: *"He was as the morning star in the midst of a cloud, and as the moon at the full; as the sun shining upon the temple of the Most High God . . . and as lilies by the rivers of waters . . . and as precious myrrh making all fragrant."*[23] Having reached a ripe old age, the saint paid his debt to human nature and, after a short bodily illness, ended his temporal life well. With joy and psalmody he passed on to eternal blessed life, escorted by holy angels and met by choirs of saints. At his burial the bishops of Lycia gathered with all the clergy and monastics and a countless multitude of people from all cities. The precious body of the saint was laid with honor in the cathedral church of the diocese of Myra on the sixth day of the month of December.[24] Many miracles were performed by the holy relics of the servant of God. For his relics gushed forth a fragrant and healing myrrh with which the sick were anointed and received healing. For this reason people from all corners of the earth came to his tomb seeking healing for their diseases and receiving it. Because not only ailments of the body, but also of the soul, were healed, and evil spirits were expelled by this holy myrrh. For the saint warred against demons and conquered them not only during his life, but also after his repose, as he conquers also now.

Several God-fearing men who lived at the mouth of the River Tanais, hearing of the myrrh-streaming and healing relics of the saint of Christ, Nicholas, which lay in Myra of Lycia, planned to sail there by sea for veneration of the relics. But the evil demon which was once cast out of the temple of Diana by St. Nicholas, seeing that the ship was being readied to sail to this great father, and being furious at the saint for the destruction of the temple and for his expulsion, plotted to prevent these men from accomplishing their planned journey and thus deprive them of holy things. He transformed himself into a woman carrying a vessel of oil, and said to them:

"I wanted to carry this container to the tomb of the saint, but I am very afraid of a sea journey because it is dangerous for a woman who is weak and suffering from a sickness of the stomach to sail on the sea. Therefore, I beg you, take this vessel, carry it to the tomb of the saint and pour oil into the lamp."

With these words the demon handed the vessel to the God-lovers. It is not known what demonic enchantments were mixed with that oil, but it was meant for the harm and destruction of the travelers. Not knowing the destructive effects of this oil, they fulfilled the request and, having taken the container, they put out to sea and sailed safely for a whole day. But in the morning a northerly wind arose and sailing became difficult for them. Being in distress during many days of unfavorable sailing, they lost patience from the continual rough seas and decided to turn back. They had already turned the ship in that direction when St. Nicholas appeared before them in a small boat and said:

"Where are you sailing to, men, and why, having abandoned your former course, are you turning back? You can calm the storm and make the journey easy for sailing. The devil's nets are hindering your voyage because the vessel of oil was given to you not by a woman, but by a demon. Throw the vessel into the sea, and immediately your voyage will begin to be successful."

Hearing this, the men threw the demonic vessel into the depths of the sea. Immediately black smoke and flames came out of it, the air was filled with a great stench, the sea opened up, the water boiled and began to bubble from the very depths, and the watery spray was like sparks of fire. Those people that stood on the ship were greatly frightened and screamed with terror, but the helper who had appeared to them commanded them to have courage and not be afraid, calmed the turbulent storm and, delivering the travelers from fear, made safe their voyage to Lycia. For at once a cool and fragrant wind blew upon them, and with gladness they successfully reached the desired city. Having venerated the the myrrh-streaming relics of their speedy helper and intercessor, they offered thanks to Almighty God and celebrated a supplicatory hymn to the great Father Nicholas. After this they returned to their own country and told everyone everywhere of that which had happened to them on their journey.

Many great and marvellous wonders were performed on land and sea by this great servant. He helped those in distress, saved from drowning and brought out those in the depths of the sea, released from captivity and brought home those who were freed, delivered from bonds and prison, defended from being wounded by the sword, freed from death and gave many healings to many, sight to the blind, power to walk to the cripple, hearing to the deaf, the gift of speech to the dumb. He enriched many suffering in infirmity and extreme poverty, gave food to the hungry, and to all those in need he appeared as a ready helper, a warm intercessor and speedy mediator and defender. And even now he helps those that call upon him and delivers them from misfortune. His miracles it is impossible to count, as it is likewise impossible to describe all of them in detail. The East and the West know this great wonderworker, and his miracles are known to all the ends of the earth. May the Triune God, the Father, Son, and Holy Spirit, be glorified in him and may his holy name be extolled by the lips of all unto the ages. Amen.

FOOTNOTES

[1] Patara was a maritime trading city in the province of Lycia (now Anatolia) in Asia Minor. It was founded by the Phoenicians and is now in ruins.

[2] Psalm 1:3.

[3] Psalm 83:11.

[4] I Corinthians 3:16.

[5] Wisdom 4:9.

[6] Psalms 24:1; 142:11; 21:10.

[7] Matthew 6:1.

[8] Matthew 6:3.

[9] It was a small church on Mt. Sion, the only one at that time in all Jerusalem, populated with heathens and bearing the name Aelia Capitolina. This church, according to tradition, was built in the house where the Lord Jesus Christ instituted the Mystery of Communion and where the Descent of the Holy Spirit upon the Apostles later occurred.

[10] Myra (now *Mira*, in Turkish *Dembre*) was the main city of ancient Lycia and was located near the sea on the River Andracus, at the mouth of which was the port of Andriaca.

[11] Matthew 5:16.

[12] I Timothy 4:12.

[13] Emperors Diocletian and Maximian (284 to 305 A.D.) were co-rulers, the first ruled in the East and the second in the West. The persecution raised by Diocletian was distinguished for its special cruelty. It began in the city of Nicomedia where, on the very day of Pascha, upwards of 20,000 Christians were burned in the church.

[14] Luke 1:69.

[15] Artemis, otherwise Diana, a famous Greek goddess personifying the moon and considered to be the protectress of forests and the hunt.

[16] Arius denied the Divinity of Jesus Christ and did not recognize His consubstantiality with the Father. Called by the Equal-of-the-Apostles Emperor Constantine, the First Ecumenical Council was convened in the year 325 under the chairmanship of the emperor himself and it introduced into Church use the Symbol of Faith, later supplemented and completed in the Second Ecumenical Council, which was held in Constantinople in 381 A.D.

[17] According to the testimony of A. N. Muraviev, there is preserved in Nicea until now, even among the Turks, a tradition concerning this. In one of the forts of this city they point out the prison of St. Nicholas. Here, according to tradition, he was imprisoned because he struck Arius at the council, and was held in bonds until he was justified by heavenly judgement, which was marked by the appearance of a Gospel and an omophorion, as they are portrayed on icons of the saint (*Letters from the East*, St. Petersburg, 1851, part I, pp. 106,107).

[18] Psalm 78:8.

[19] Psalm 34:11,12.

[20] Matthew 8:26.

[21] John 14:12.

[22] I Corinthians 3:16,17.

[23] Ecclesiasticus 50:6-8.

[24.]The year of the death of St. Nicholas is not known precisely; according to some, the servant of God died in the year 341, but according to others, the year of his demise occurred between the years 345 - 352 A.D.

The Miracles of Saint Nicholas

Which Occurred after His Death

St. Nicholas performed many miracles not only during his lifetime, but also after his death. Who would not be astonished to hear of his wonderful miracles! For not only one country or region but the whole earth is filled with the miracles of St. Nicholas. Go to the Greeks, and there they marvel at them; go to the Latins — and there they are astonished at them, and in Syria they extol them. Throughout the whole world they are amazed at St. Nicholas. Come to Russia and you will see that there is neither city nor village where there is not a multitude of the miracles of St. Nicholas.

In the time of the Greek Emperor Leo and Patriarch Athanasius the following illustrious miracle of St. Nicholas was performed.[1] At midnight, the great Nicholas, Archbishop of Myra, appeared in a vision to a certain pious old man, a lover of the poor and hospitable to strangers, by the name of Theophanes, and said:

"Awake, Theophanes, rise and go to the iconographer Aggaeus and order him to paint three icons: our Saviour Jesus Christ the Lord, Who created heaven and earth and fashioned man; the most pure Lady Theotokos and intercessor for the race of Christians; Nicholas, Archbishop of Myra, for I should reveal myself at Constantinople. When these three icons have been painted, present them to the patriarch and the whole council. Go quickly and do not disobey."

Having said this, the saint disappeared. Having awakened from sleep, that God-loving man Theophanes, being frightened at the vision, at once went to the iconographer Aggaeus and begged him to paint three large icons: Christ the Saviour, the most pure Theotokos, and St. Nicholas. By the will of the merciful Saviour, His most pure Mother, and

St. Nicholas, Aggaeus painted three icons and brought them to Theophanes. The latter took the icons, placed them in the chamber, and said to his wife:

"Let us serve a dinner in our house and pray to God about our sins."

She agreed with joy. Theophanes went to the market, bought food and drink for thirty gold coins and, bringing it home, arranged a splendid meal for the patriarch. Afterwards he went to the patriarch and invited him and the whole council, that he would bless his house and partake of food and drink. The patriarch consented, came with the council to the home of Theophanes and, going into the chamber, saw the three icons standing there: on one the image of our Lord Jesus Christ; on the other, the most pure Theotokos; and on the third, St. Nicholas. Approaching the first icon, the patriarch said:

"Glory to Thee, O Christ God, Who hast fashioned all creation. It was fitting to paint this image."

Then, approaching the second icon, he said:

"It is good that this image of the most holy Theotokos and intercessor for the whole world was painted."

Coming to the third icon, the patriarch said:

"This is an image of Nicholas, archbishop of Myra. It was improper to depict him on such a large icon. He was the son of simple people, Theophanes and Nonna, who were peasants by origin."

Calling for the master of the house, the patriarch said to him:

"Theophanes, do not order Aggaeus to paint an image of Nicholas of such large size."

And he commanded him to take away the image of the saint, saying:

"He is not worthy to stand with Christ and the Most Pure One."

The pious man Theophanes, with great sadness removing the icon of St. Nicholas from the chamber, placed it in an honourable place in a storeroom, and, choosing from the cathedral clergy a wonderful and prudent man named Callistus, he asked him to stand before the icon and magnify St. Nicholas. He himself was very saddened by the words of the patriarch, who ordered the icon of St. Nicholas to be removed from the room. But in the Scriptures it says: *Them that glorify Me I will glorify.*[2]. Thus said the Lord Jesus Christ, by Whom, as we shall see, the saint himself was to be glorified.

Glorifying God and the Most Pure One, the patriarch sat down at the table with all his council, and there was a meal. After it the patriarch stood up, magnified God and the Most Pure One and, drinking wine, rejoiced together with all his council. And during that time Callistus glorified and magnified the great hierarch St. Nicholas. But here there was a shortage of wine, and the patriarch and his escort wished to drink still and make glad. And one of the group said:

"Theophanes, bring more wine for the patriarch and make the dinner pleasant."

He replied: "There is no more wine, my lord, and already the market is closed, and there is nowhere to buy it."

In sadness he recalled how St. Nicholas appeared to him in a vision and commanded the three icons to be painted: the Saviour, the most pure Mother of God, and himself. Secretly entering the storeroom, he fell down before the image of the saint and with tears said:

"O holy Nicholas! Thy birth was wondrous and thy life holy; thou healest many of the ailing. I entreat thee, show now a miracle for me an evil one, and increase the wine for me."

Having said this and having blessed himself, he went to where the wine vessels stood; and through the prayers of the holy wonderworker Nicholas these vessels were full of wine. Taking wine joyfully, Theophanes brought it to the patriarch. He drank and praised, saying:

"Never have I drank such wine before."

And the drinkers said that Theophanes had kept the best wine to the end of the feast. But he kept secret the most marvelous miracle of St. Nicholas.

With joy the patriarch and council went away to the house near St. Sophia's. In the morning there came to the patriarch a certain nobleman by the name of Theodore, from the village of Sierdal, from the island of Myra, and begged the patriarch to go with him, for one of his daughters was possessed by a demon of sickness, and read the Holy Gospel over her head. The patriarch agreed, took the Gospel, went aboard the ship with all his council and set sail. When they were in the open sea, a tempest of powerful billows arose, the ship capsized, and all fell into the water and swam, crying out and imploring God, the most pure Theotokos, and St. Nicholas. And the most pure Theotokos prayed to her Son, our Saviour Jesus Christ, for the council so that the ranks of clergy not perish. Then the ship righted itself and, through the mercy of God, the entire council got into it again. While sinking, Patriarch Athanasius remembered his sin before St. Nicholas, and, crying out, he prayed and said:

"O great hierarch of Christ, Archbishop of Myra, Nicholas the Wonderworker! I have sinned before thee, forgive and have mercy on me a sinner and wretch, save me from the depths of the sea, from this bitter hour, and from sudden death."

O marvellous wonder! the haughty was brought low, and the humble was wondrously exalted and worthily glorified.

Suddenly St. Nicholas appeared, walking on the sea, as on dry land, drew near to the patriarch and took him by the hand with the words:

"Athanasius, has it become necessary that in the abyss of the sea thou hast need of help from me who sprang from common people?"

And he, barely in a condition to open his mouth, exhausted, said with bitter weeping:

"O St. Nicholas, great hierarch, quick to help, remember not mine evil arrogance, deliver me from this sudden death in the depths of the sea, and I will glorify thee all the days of my life."

And the saint said to him: "Fear not, brother, here Christ delivers thee by my hand. Sin thou no more, lest worse things befall thee. Enter thy ship.

Having said this, St. Nicholas took the patriarch from the water and put him on the ship, with the words:

"Thou art saved, go back to thy duties in Constantinople."

And the saint vanished.

Seeing the patriarch, all cried aloud: "Glory to Thee, O Christ Saviour, and to thee, O most pure Queen and Lady Theotokos, who have delivered our master from drowning."

As if awaking from sleep, the patriarch asked them: "Where am I, brethren?"

"On thy ship, master," they replied, "and we are all unharmed."

Beginning to weep, the patriarch said: "Brethren, I have sinned before St. Nicholas, truly he is great: he walked on the sea as on dry land, took me by the hand and placed me on the ship; indeed he is quick to help all that call upon him with faith."

The ship swiftly sailed back to Constantinople. Leaving the ship with all the council, the patriarch tearfully went to the church of St. Sophia and sent for Theophanes, bidding him to bring at once the wonderful icon of St. Nicholas. When Theophanes brought the icon, the patriarch fell down before it with tears and said:

"I have sinned, O St. Nicholas, forgive me a sinner."

Having said this, he took the icon in his hands, kissed it reverently together with the council and carried it away to the church of St. Sophia. Next day he laid the foundation in Constantinople for a stone church in the name of St. Nicholas. When the church was erected, the patriarch himself consecrated it on the day of the commemoration of St. Nicholas. And the saint healed on that day forty ailing men and women. After that the patriarch gave thirty litres of gold and many villages and farms for the adornment of the church. And he built near it a honorable monastery. And many came there: the blind, the halt, and lepers. Having touched this icon of St. Nicholas, they all went away healthy, glorifying God and His wonderworker.

In Constantinople there lived a certain man named Nicholas, who lived by handicraft. Being pious, he made a pledge never to pass through the day consecrated to the memory of St. Nicholas without remembrance of the God-pleaser. This he kept unfailingly, according to the words of the Scripture: *Honour the Lord by thy righteous labours,*[3] and always firmly remembered this. Thus he reached ripe old age and, not having strength to work, fell on hard times. The day of the memory of St. Nicholas drew near, and here, pondering to himself what to do about it, the old man said to his wife:

"The honourable day of the great hierarch of Christ, Nicholas, is coming; how can we poor ones celebrate this day in our poverty?"

The pious wife answered her husband: "Thou knowest, my lord, that the end of our life is near, for old age has overtaken both thee and me; even if we have now come to the end of our life, do not change thy vows and do not forget about thy love for the saint."

She showed her carpet to her husband and said: "Take the carpet, go and sell it and buy all things necessary for the worthy celebration to the memory of St. Nicholas. We have nothing else, and we don't need this carpet, for we have no children to whom this could be left."

Hearing this, the pious old man praised his wife and, taking the carpet, left. When he came to the square, where stands the column of the emperor St. Constantine the Great, and was passing by the church of St. Plato, he met the always-ready-to-help St. Nicholas in the form of an honorable elder, and he said to bearer of the carpet:

"Dear friend, where are you going?"

"It is necessary for me to go to the market," replied the other.

Coming closer, St. Nicholas said:

"A good thing. But tell me for how much thou wishest to sell this carpet, for I would like to buy thy carpet."

The old man said to the saint: "This carpet at one time was bought for eight gold coins, but now I will take for it whatever thou givest me."

The saint said to the old man: "Would you agree to take six gold coins for it?"

"If you give me so much," said the old man, "I will take it with joy."

St. Nicholas put his hand into the pocket of his garment, took gold from there and, giving six large gold coins into the hand of the old man, said to him:

"Take this, friend, and give me the carpet."

The old man gladly took the gold, for the carpet was worth less than that. Taking the carpet from the hand of the old man, St. Nicholas went away. When they parted, those present on the square said to the old man:

"Are you seeing apparitions, old man, that you alone converse with?"

For they saw only the old man and heard his voice, and the saint was invisible and inaudible for them. Meanwhile St. Nicholas came with the carpet to the wife of the old man and said to her:

"Thy husband, my old friend, meeting me, he turned to me with this request: 'If thou lovest me, take this carpet to my wife, because if is necessary for me to carry another thing, and do thou guard it like thine own.' "

Having said this, the saint became invisible. Seeing this honourable man, who shone with light, and taking from him the carpet, the wife out of fear did not dare to ask who he was. Thinking that her husband had forgotten his words spoken to her, and his love for the saint, the wife became angry with her husband and said:

"Woe is poor me, my husband is a transgressor and full of lies!"

Saying these words and others similar to them, burning with love toward the saint, she did not wish even to look at the carpet.

Not knowing about what had happened, her husband bought all that was necessary for the celebration day in memory of St. Nicholas and was walking to his cottage, rejoicing in the sale of the carpet and that it made it unnecessary to depart from his pious custom. When he came home, his indignant wife met him with evil words:

"Henceforth go away from me, for thou hast lied to St. Nicholas. Truly said Christ, the Son of God: *No man, having put his hand to the plow, and looking back, is fit for the kingdom of God.*[4]

Having said these words and others similar to them, she brought the carpet to her husband and said:

"Here, take it, but thou shalt never see me again; thou hast lied to St. Nicholas and, therefore thou shalt lose all that thou shalt achieve by the celebration of his memory. For it is written: *If a man shall keep the whole law, and yet offend in one, he is guilty of all.*"[5]

Hearing this from his wife and seeing his carpet, the old man was astonished and could not find words to answer his wife. For a long while he stood and finally he understood that St. Nicholas had performed a miracle. Sighing from the depths of his heart and being filled with joy, he lifted up his hands towards heaven and said:

"Glory to Thee, O Christ God, Who hast wrought wonders through St. Nicholas!"

And the old man said to his wife: "For the sake of the fear of God, tell me, who brought you this carpet, a man or a woman, an old man or a youth?

His wife replied: "A radiant old man, honorable, clothed in bright garments, brought us this carpet and said to me: 'Thy husband is my friend, and so, meeting me, he asked me to carry this carpet to thee, take it.' Having taken the carpet, I did not dare to ask the one who came who he was, seeing him shining with light."

Hearing that from his wife, the old man wondered and showed her the portion of gold left over and all the things bought by him for the celebration of the day in memory of St. Nicholas: the victuals, wine, prosphora, and candles.

"The Lord liveth!" he exclaimed. "The man who bought the carpet from me and brought it back to the house of us paupers and lowly servants, indeed it is St. Nicholas, for a man who saw me in conversation with him said: 'Do you see an apparition?' They saw only me, but he was invisible."

Then both the old man and his wife exclaimed, sending up thanksgiving to Almighty God and praise to the great bishop of Christ, Nicholas, the speedy helper of all that call upon him with faith. Being filled with joy, they went at once to the church of St. Nicholas, bearing gold and the carpet, and made known to all the clergy and all who were there concerning what had happened to them. And all the people, hearing their story, glorified God and St. Nicholas who worketh mercy for His servants. Afterwards they sent to Patriarch Michael[6] and told him everything. The patriarch commanded that the old man be given an allowance from the property of the church of St. Sophia. And they made an honourable feast, with the sending up of praises and the singing of hymns.

There lived in Constantinople a pious man by the name of Epiphanius. He was very wealthy and honored with great respect by Emperor Constantine,[7] and had many slaves. One day he wished to buy a youth to serve him and on the third day of the month of December, taking a litre of gold in seventy-two gold coins, he mounted a horse and went to the marketplace where merchants, newcomers from Russia, sell slaves. He was unable to buy a slave, and he returned home. Dismounting the horse, he entered his palace, removed the gold which he had taken to the market from his pocket and placed it somewhere in the palace and forgot where he put it. This befell him from the perpetual evil enemy, the devil, who unceasingly makes war on the race of Christians, so that honor will flourish on the earth [i.e., Christians will triumph over the devil, although that is not his intention when he makes war against them — ed.]. Not being able to bear the piety of this man, he intended to cast him into the depths of sin. Next morning the nobleman called a youth who was servant to him, and said:

"Bring me the gold which I gave thee yesterday, it is necessary for me to go to the marketplace."

Hearing this, the servant was frightened, for the master had not given the gold to him, and he said: "You did not give the gold to me, Master."

The master said: "O evil and lying head, tell me, where didst thou put the gold given to thee by me?"

He, not having anything, swore that he did not understand what his master was saying to him. The nobleman became angry and ordered the servants to bind the youth, beat him without mercy, and put him in irons.

And he said to himself: "I will decide his fate when the feast of St. Nicholas is past," for this feast had to be the next day.

The imprisoned one, the youth, with tears cried out to Almighty God, Who delivers all in misfortune:

"O Lord my God, Jesus Christ, Almighty One, Son of the living God,

Who dwellest in light unapproachable, I cry unto Thee, for Thou knowest the heart of man, do Thou, the helper of orphans, the deliverance of those in misfortune, the consolation of the afflicted, deliver me from this danger from an unknown source. Cause merciful deliverance so that also my master, having been delivered from sin and unrighteousness because of me, will glorify Thee with gladness of heart, and so that I, Thy wicked servant, delivered from this danger, unjustly come upon me, may exalt Thee in thanksgiving for Thy love for mankind."

Saying this with tears and such like, adding prayer to prayer and tears to tears, the youth cried to St. Nicholas:

"O honourable Father St. Nicholas, deliver me from calamity! Thou knowest that I am innocent of that which my master accuses me of. Tomorrow will be thy feastday, and I am in great distress."

Night came, and the exhausted youth fell asleep. And St. Nicholas, always quick to help all that call upon him with faith, appeared to him and said:

"Grieve not: Christ will deliver thee through me His servant."

Immediately the irons fell off his feet, and he arose and sent up praise to God and St. Nicholas. At that same hour the saint appeared also to his master, and reproached him: "Why art thou unjust to thy servant, Epiphanius? thou thyself art guilty, for thou didst forget where thou didst place the gold, and the youth thou dost torture is guiltless, and he is faithful to thee. But as thou thyself didst not design this, and wast taught by the primordial evil enemy, the devil, thus I also appear to thee so that thy love for God will not cease. Arise and release the youth: and if thou disobey me, then great misfortune will befall thee."

Then, pointing his finger to the place where lay the gold, St. Nicholas said: "Arise, take thy gold and release the youth."

Having said this, he became invisible.

The nobleman Epiphanius awoke with trembling, went to the place in the palace indicated to him by the saint, and found the gold put there by himself. Then, seized with fear and filled with joy, he said:

"Glory to Thee, O Christ God, the hope of all the race of Christians; glory to Thee, the hope of the hopeless, the speedy consolation of the despairing; glory to Thee Who hast shown light to the whole world and speedy upraising to those fallen in sin, St. Nicholas, who healeth not only bodily ailments but also temptations of the soul."

All in tears he fell before the honorable image of St. Nicholas and said:

"I thank thee, honorable Father, for thou didst save me the unworthy and sinful one, and came to me, an evil one, cleansing me of sin. What shall I render unto thee, for thou didst take care of me, coming to me."

Having said this and like things, the nobleman came to the youth, and seeing that the irons had fallen from him, he fell into yet greater awe and reproached himself very much. He commanded the youth to be released at once and he alleviated him in every way; he himself watched the whole night through, giving thanks to God and St. Nicholas who delivered him from such a sin. When the bells began to ring for Matins, he stood up, took the gold and went with the youth to the church of St. Nicholas. Here he joyfully related to all what mercy God and St. Nicholas had bestowed upon him. And all glorified God Who worketh such miracles through His servants. When Matins was finished, the master said to the young man in church: "Child, it was not me a sinner, but Thy God, the Maker of heaven and earth, and His holy servant Nicholas, that freed thee from slavery, so that some day I will be forgiven for the injustice which I, unknowingly, did to thee."

Having said this, he divided the gold into three portions: the first portion he gave to the church of St. Nicholas, the second to the poor, and the third he gave to the youth, saying:

"Take this, child, and thou shalt be in debt to no one except only to St. Nicholas. And I will care for thee as a child-loving father."

Giving thanks to God and St. Nicholas, Epiphanius joyfully went to his home.

Once upon a time in Kiev, on the day in memory of the martyrs Boris and Gleb, a multitude of people flocked from all the cities and villages for the feast of the holy martyrs. One Kievan, having great faith in St. Nicholas and in the holy martyrs Boris and Gleb, took a boat and sailed to Vishegorod, to venerate the tomb of the holy martyrs Boris and Gleb,[8] taking with him candles, incense, and prosphora — everything necessary for a worthy celebration. Having venerated the relics of the saints and having rejoiced in spirit, he departed for home. When he sailed on the river Dnieper, his wife, holding her child in her arms, fell asleep and dropped the child into the water, and he drowned. His father, began to tear his hair, crying aloud:

"Woe is me, St. Nicholas, for I did not have great enough faith in thee that thou mightest save my child from drowning! Who will be heir to my property; whom shall I teach to make radiant festivity to thy memory, my protector? How shall I proclaim thy great kindness, which thou hast poured out on the whole world and on me the unfortunate, when my child is drowned? I wanted to raise him, enlightening him with thy miracles so that after my death he would praise me because my offspring keeps the memory of St. Nicholas. But thou, O saint, hast not only given me sorrow, but also to thyself, for soon it will be necessary for commemoration of thee to cease in my house, for I an old and await the end. If thou hadst wished to save the child, thou couldst have saved him, but thou thyself didst allow him to drawn, and didst not deliver mine only child from the sea deeps. Or dost thou think that I do not know of thy miracles? For they are innumerable, and the tongue of man cannot relate them, and I, holy Father, believe that with thee all things are possible that thou desirest to do, but overcome mine iniquities. Now I understand, tormented with sorrow, that if I had kept the commandments of God blamelessly, all creation would be subject to me, as to Adam in paradise before the fall. But now all creation revolts against me: water drowns, wild beasts attack, serpents swallow, lightning burns, the birds consume, animals rage and trample everything, people destroy, bread given us for food does not satisfy us and, by the will of God, will be unto us for ruination. And we, endowed with soul and intelligence and created in the image of God, do not fulfill, however, as required, the will of our Creator. But be not angered against me, holy Father Nicholas, that I dare to speak boldly, for I do not despair of my salvation, having thee as helper."

And his wife tore her hair and beat herself on the cheeks. Finally they reached the city and in sorrow came to their home. Night came, and then the bishop of Christ, Nicholas, who is quick to help all that call upon him, performed a wondrous miracle, such as never in olden times. During the night he took from the river the drowned child and placed him in the choir loft of the church of St. Sophia, alive and unharmed. When the time came for morning prayers, the sacristan entered the church and heard a child crying in the choir loft. And he stood a long while wondering: "Who has allowed a woman into the choir loft?"

He went to the one in charge of the choir and began to reprimand him; that one replied that he knew nothing, but the sacristan accused him: "You are caught in the act, for children cry in the choir loft."

The one in charge of the choir was frightened and, going up to the lock, he saw that it was untouched and heard a child's voice. Entering the choir loft, he saw before the icon of St. Nicholas a child, all soaking wet with water. Not knowing how to explain it, he told the metropolitan about it. Having finished the morning service, the metropolitan sent to gather the people in the square and asked them whose child lay in the choir loft of the church of St. Sophia. All the citizens went into the church, wondering how this child came to be in the choir loft, wet with water. The father of the child came also, in order to wonder at the miracle, and, seeing, recognized him. But, not trusting himself, he went to his wife and told her all in detail. And she at once began to reproach her husband, saying:

"How is it that thou dost not understand that this is a miracle performed by St. Nicholas?"

She went with haste to the church, recognized her child, and, not touching him, fell down before the icon of St. Nicholas and prayed, with compunction and tears. Her husband, standing at a distance, shed tears. Hearing about this, all the people flocked to see the miracle, and the whole city gathered, glorifying God and St. Nicholas. The metropolitan celebrated an honorable feast, as observed on the commemoration day of St. Nicholas, glorifying the Holy Trinity, the Father, the Son, and the Holy Spirit. Amen.

---

[1] This was in the middle of the 8th century, during the reign of Leo the Isaurian.

[2] I Kings (I Samuel) 2:30.

[3] Proverbs 3:9.

[4] Luke 9:62.

[5] Cf. James 2:10.

[6] Michael Cerularius, 1043 to 1058 A.D.

[7] Constantine Monomach, of course, who reigned from 1042 to 1060 A.D.

[8] The relics of Sts. Boris and Gleb were then still in Vishegorod of Kiev. The miracle which is related here occurred between the years 1087 and 1091.

This is a complete translation of the *Life* and the *Miracles* of St. Nicholas as it appears in *THE LIVES OF THE SAINTS in the Russian Language as set forth according to the guidance of the Menologion of St. Dimitry of Rostov*, Moscow, Synodal Press, 1903.